Thomas and Eliza Little

Irish Pioneers in India
and Western Australia
1797 - 1877

Stephen Lally

Front cover illustration

"A view of Koombana Bay on Port Leschenault, Australind, Western Australia drawn and lithographed by T.C. Dibdin, from an original sketch taken on the spot by Miss Louisa Clifton.   c.1840".
Reproduced with permission of the National Library of Australia.

www.lally.org.uk

To my grandchildren

This book is written to tell you who you are and where you have come from. It describes historical facts and situations that illustrate the lives of our family and how your flesh and blood lived 200 years ago. It shows the incredible contrasts between your ancestors' lives and the lives you lead today.

The book is also dedicated to the grandchildren of all the Irish who left for new lands over many years.

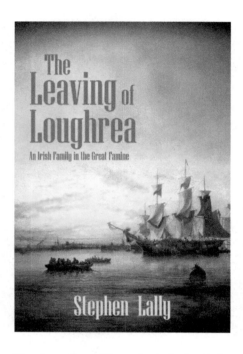

By the same author

The Leaving of Loughrea is based on Eliza's younger brother, Patrick, and other members of the Lally family between 1818 and 1848. It could just as easily be your story if you have ancestors who were among over a million people who left the beautiful and tragic land of Ireland in the 1840s. This family lived in the Loughrea area, County Galway, Ireland, and their story is similar to that of so many Irish families as they struggled against the odds, were overwhelmed by the tragedy of the Great Famine, and were forced to leave their beloved homeland. This story explores how the Irish lived at this time, how they thought, and the reasons for their situation in Ireland. It brings together the many strands of Irish society; the economics, politics, and philosophy that dominated their lives. It describes the terrible journeys that members of the family undertook to reach England, America, Canada, and Australia.

CONTENTS

INTRODUCTION

I write this book as if I am explaining the situation to my grandchildren. I only have five grandchildren and I hope more than that number of people will read this story but I have found with previous books that writing with them in mind forces me to simplify the tale and make it easily understood. In particular, it emphasises the enormous differences between their young lives today and the lives described in this book.

This is the story of some of my ancestors and it has a specific objective of describing the detail of their lives, how they lived and what they experienced. I want you, my reader, to *feel and understand* how they lived and I cannot achieve this without painting a much broader picture than just their births, marriages and deaths. I want to tell you about what they did and why, how they felt and what their attitudes were 200 years ago and to contrast this with activities and attitudes today. The world was a very different place then and I want you to empathise.

This is not a detailed history of Ireland, the British in India or the settlement of Western Australia. If this book makes you want to know more, then you will find a few suggestions in my small bibliography at the end. I have carried out a great deal of original research, helped enormously by friends in Ireland and Western Australia and much of the background comes from the books listed at the end. I am indebted to these authors for the depth of their knowledge.

Nearly all surviving documents and memories relate to Thomas. It was a man's world and he became a great man. But what of Eliza? I'm biased towards her as she is my great-great-great-aunt. I don't believe Thomas could have been as successful as he was without the support of Eliza. I want to bring her out of the shadows.

I researched this book in the wrong order because that's how the opportunities arose. Research into India, the middle of the story, was left to the end because the British Library, the source of nearly all that information, was closed due to covid. By the time I had all the facts (or as many as I could reasonably obtain) I had a strong feeling for Thomas and Eliza. I felt I knew them. So I started again at the beginning and re-wrote much of the story because I felt I could draw conclusions from the many facts, make assumptions. But assumptions can be dangerous. My image of Thomas is of a forceful, principled and kind gentleman. I picture Eliza as being hard working too, and fun; a woman in her own right but a strong support to Thomas. They were a team; partners in their many adventures. My assumptions are the glue that holds the facts together and makes their story. I think I'm right because, other than criticism of their Catholicism, I have read nothing other than good things about them.

Where did this story come from?

Eliza Little was my great-great-great-aunt, born Elizabeth Lally but known as Eliza. She was 21 years older than her youngest brother, Patrick Lally. Patrick was my great-great-grandfather.

Patrick Lally, left Ireland in the 1840s, when he was in his twenties and went to London. He was successful for a while when he had a mushroom nursery in Kensington. But he fell on hard times. He split up with his wife and some of his family and ended his days in Kensington Workhouse. His life in Ireland is described in my book *The Leaving of Loughrea* (pronounced Loch-ray). There is a Lally family story, passed down the generations, that Patrick always talked about his great missed opportunity in the Swan River Colony but the detail was lost over time. It was about a vineyard there. Did he send an agent there who ran off with the money or did he just make an investment that failed? Did he know somebody there? For an old man, hard up on his luck, it seemed to be an "if only" story. If only he hadn't lost his money. If only he'd gone there, he would have been a great success. If only!

Just an old man's dreams? But there was enough detail to make it interesting. It must have meant something. Why specifically Swan River? Why specifically a vineyard? Who was his contact or agent?

I mentioned this in *The Leaving of Loughrea*, in a summary of Patrick's later life. One day I received an email from Linda Sue, née Little, in California, who noticed too many coincidences for there not to be a link between her family and mine; The Swan River, vineyards, Patrick's mother's maiden name, Loughrea, and others. It didn't take long for the link to be verified and I found I had a new and exciting relation in Eliza.

The more I discovered about Eliza and her husband and their brothers, the more fascinated I became and this story grew from there. Poor Patrick, as he sat in the workhouse must have dreamed of what might have been. He dreamt of his 'wealthy sister' and if only he had gone to her. At the time that Thomas Little was helping poor Irish people, some from London, settle in Australia, Patrick was probably quite successful and optimistic for his future in London. He had a large family and a business so, when Eliza wrote to tell him about her life, as she must have done, he didn't go. If only!

My grandfather, Will Lally, must have been intrigued by his grandfather's, Patrick's, story and must have had more detail. He wrote to Western Australia in 1952 to enquire about the name Liddle and wine making. (See the copy on page 4) Unfortunately, the London accent pronounces a T as a D and, as the story had no doubt been passed to him verbally, he got the name wrong. If he'd asked about Little and wine making we might have known this story years ago. If only!

Eliza Little, at the end of her life, gave the final piece of evidence, if any more was needed, linking her to the Elizabeth Lally in Ireland and to the train of events that make up her story. Her death certificate gave her maiden name – Lally.

An advert for sailings to Swan River in the Illustrated London News of 24th December 1853. The colony was still referred to as Swan River as late as this.

honest profit.

Observe.—Every purchaser of the " Pianista " should strictly observe that the addresses, 5, Conduit-street, Regent-street, and 67, Paternoster-row, are on the pink wrapper of each Number; and they should order through Booksellers, or send direct

" The arrangement of these Operas for Piano are the finest in Europe."—Atlas.

FOR SWAN RIVER.—Will have immediate despatch, the splendid fast-sailing Ship TREVANCORE, A 1, 600 tons; T. BROWNE, Commander. Loading in the London Docks. This ship has superior accommodation for passengers.
For freight or passage apply to WILLIAM FELGATE and Co., 4, Clement's-lane, Lombard-street.

WALTHEW'S "LIVERPOOL" LINE of AUSTRALIAN PACKETS. Established in 1848.

Ships.	Tons.	Destination.	To sail.
THEMIS	1800	MELBOURNE	1st January.
BALMORAL	1750	SYDNEY	1st January.
JAMES CARSON	2000	MELBOURNE	10th January.

These A 1 Clipper-ships land Goods and Passengers on the wharf free of charge.

The reply to my grandfather's letter enquiring about his mysterious ancestors in Western Australia.

What made Thomas and Eliza exceptional?

Cecil Woodham-Smith in his book, *The Great Hunger,* stated that the conditions to which the Irish poor had been subjected for centuries gave them such a great handicap that very few first-generation emigrants from Ireland ever made a success of their lives. Wherever they went, their Irish accent and Catholicism condemned them to be treated with aversion and contempt. Thomas and Eliza were exceptions because they rose above this and, as first-generation Irish emigrants in India and Australia, they achieved success. They left their mark and it was a mark for good.

They took bold steps. They married, to a certain extent, against the rules. Nobody else would do. They emigrated to India and their success there cannot have been achieved without taking risky decisions. They moved on to another new life in Australia and left a fairly secure employer there to branch out on their own. They were ambitious, forceful and courageous enough to cross a series of thresholds, some sudden, some gradual, but doorways into new lives nevertheless. Where did they get that courage?

You cannot judge the past by today's standards.

Our story starts in the reign of King George III and Thomas and Eliza left Ireland in the reign of William IV. They left India five months after Queen Victoria came to the throne. The years before they left Ireland were relatively peaceful in England as major wars had ended, usually with British victory. The Battle of Trafalgar was won in 1805. War against America and the Peninsula Wars ended in 1814, and Waterloo put an end to Napoleon's empire in 1815. This left Britain as unchallenged master of the world's seas and led to accelerating growth of industrial power at home and the British Empire abroad. The adult lives of Thomas and Eliza cover this period of Britain's most dramatic growth. They hardly benefitted from this in Ireland but were in the thick of these developments in their later lives.

Despite all this glory, Thomas' and Eliza's lives were dreadful by our modern standards, although not by their own standards of the time. Their living conditions were clearly accepted, if not acceptable, in their day. There was no clean water, no gas or electricity and no quick and easy means of communication. There were no cures for most serious diseases. Attitudes to marriage and death were so very different to those of today. Our living standards in the West today, with secure housing, heating, a vast range of foods unimaginable to our forebears and even the money to buy this book, are the standards enjoyed by kings of 200 years ago. Thomas and Eliza were not any less happy than we are because they had so little. Even happiness is relative and nobody told them how poor they were by our standards. They knew no different. Theirs was an age of very few rights and many responsibilities. Nowadays, the government is harangued almost daily for seriously letting down some region, group of people, industry or interest group, but it was not until the middle of the 19th century that it began to be accepted as the job of parliament to interfere with people's lives in such ways. You were on your own without a safety net. Having few rights yourself perhaps led to little thought being given to the rights of others, humans or animals.

In my research I have sometimes felt that my secondary sources stress the bad aspects of life, perhaps because they were most memorable and most reported at the time but also because they are shocking news to 21st century readers. What we consider to have been bad times were probably accepted without thought, as normal then. There must have been happy times and for every ship that met with some problem or disaster there were several that had a smooth voyage. For every bad day in the barracks, there must have been a good time relaxing. By the nature of the resources available, this story can only describe the highlights in Thomas' and Eliza's lives. Remember as you read, that for every incident or every day I describe, there were a hundred days of routine and, perhaps, boredom, as in every life, but also times for singing and dancing.

Whatever I write here will be controversial because, as I write, it has become fashionable among a minority to criticise everything to do with Empire as colonialist and racist which, of course, it was. But you cannot wish the past away or change it by yelling about it now. I want to ignore all this politics in my simple story so if you feel I should have criticised more aspects of Thomas' and Eliza's lives and times you will be disappointed. I have tried to present life as it was for them and how they thought then, without any modern judgement.

Thomas and Eliza were certainly good people who made great sacrifices to give their fellow men and women better lives. So let us learn about them as the flawed humans that we all are, so that they may rest in peace and we can celebrate the great contribution they made at their moment in history.

IRELAND

CHAPTER 1

TWO FAMILIES

It was Wednesday 1st January 1800 in a small hamlet near the market town of Loughrea in County Galway in the west of Ireland. It was not just the start of a new year but the threshold of a new century when all across Ireland people were praying for new opportunities and better times in the future.

A baby boy was born on this auspicious day, crossing the threshold into a new life. He was Thomas, the first child of Robert and Judith Little who had been married for eighteen months. There would have been great urgency to have Thomas baptised, to place the boy in God's safe hands against all the troubles and dangers in this world and beyond. Infant mortality was high and if the child had died unbaptised his soul would not be allowed into heaven and would have wandered for eternity in limbo.

Somebody would have been sent off across the fields within minutes of Thomas' arrival to call the priest and then spread the good news to the family. Perhaps Judith's sister, Annie Lally, had been with her during the confinement and may have brought her own tiny children with her. The youngest, William, may have only been a few months old and Eliza Lally was only 2½ years old. Eliza would have

J T Reilly in his 'Reminiscences of Fifty Years Residence in Western Australia', published in 1903, states Thomas' birth as 1st January 1800 in Co. Galway. Reilly arrived in WA in 1851 and would have known Thomas for up to 26 years and is quite specific about his birth date and made a point of mentioning it.

been delighted to be one of the first to see the new baby and fascinated to see him bathed and fed. When the priest arrived she would have seen the sign of the cross placed upon Thomas' head and she might have been allowed to hold the new baby. A second duty of the priest was to 'church' the new mother. This was to praise and thank God that the mother was well. It was to cleanse her after childbirth and to welcome her back into the church as she would have been given dispensation from attending mass in the final weeks of her pregnancy.

There may have been one cloud casting a shadow over this happy event. It is almost certain that Robert Little was a Protestant and Judith, née Brett, was a Catholic and this would have been difficult for some members of both families to accept. For Judith's priest to have permitted such a marriage, Robert would have agreed that all their children would be christened and brought up as Catholics and this may have created tension with some members of Robert's family.

However, many family members and friends would have visited the Littles to congratulate Judith and to share her relief that she had successfully endured her first birth. Others would have wished them all well on that first Sunday when they got together for the

An illicit Mass in a ruined church. The man on the left is on the lookout for police who may break up the illegal Catholic gathering.

mass. Along with the wonder of any first child, the admiring looks and flattery of mother and child, and the father too, there must have been many a comment on the significance of the day of Thomas' birth. Robert and Judith must have been regaled with,

"To be sure, God's placed him here for a reason. He'll be a great man."

"Ay, he'll be a grand boy when he grows up"

Can a man's date of birth affect his life? Yes, if he was born on 1st January 1800, an auspicious date right at the start of a new century, a time of new beginnings and hope for a better future.

"Come on, lad, this is your century, you're going to change the world".

Words like that ringing in Thomas' ears from childhood could perhaps have created his ambition, sense of purpose and his destiny. In the closing lines of an old Gaelic Christening prayer – and don't forget that they were all speaking Gaelic – the priest and congregation would have prayed;

> *Dearest Father in heaven . . . . .*
> *Teach this child to follow in Your footsteps*
> *And to live in the ways of*
> *Love, Faith, Hope and Charity.   Amen.*

It can safely be said that this prayer was granted and these four ways of life best describe Thomas, and Eliza, his future wife, and are as good an explanation as any of their future happiness and success.

The scene has been set for the life of Thomas Little and Eliza Lally; their one life together, their future success, amid the constant background of discrimination.

It is to be twenty years before surviving records allow us to pick up their lives again in detail but somehow the Littles and Lallys survived and their families grew. Among the poverty of Ireland the children were given an education which was most likely received in 'hedge schools' run by Catholic priests in barns, houses or even under hedges if there was nowhere else. One of Eliza's younger brothers, Michael, was a clerk in later life so it was a good education too, teaching them to read and write and do arithmetic. The concept of childhood, as we know it today, was unknown and almost as soon as they could walk children were given tasks such as searching the fields for missed potatoes or helping to gather in the flax. Everybody had to contribute to the family.

Both our families, the Littles and the Lallys, lived in hamlets around the market town of Loughrea. This area in the east of County Galway was a fertile land of low hills with arable and livestock farming and market gardens so it fared better than the rough and rocky land to the west. Because of the pleasant scenery and climate there were about forty large houses around Loughrea, each with its garden and essential kitchen garden to provide vegetables for the house. But this is the sort of description one would see in a tourist guide and it ignores the mass of tumble-down shacks, dotted everywhere, in which the great majority of people lived, scratching a living out of the poorer land.

Loughrea was one of the biggest towns in Connaught, a market town on the main road between Dublin and the city of Galway. It was largely owned by the Earl of Clanricarde, the largest landowner in the county. The rapid growth of the population in the early 1800s meant that Loughrea grew from about 3,000 inhabitants in 1800 to about 5,500 in 1841. In their youth Thomas and Eliza knew Loughrea well and would have visited it regularly. There were two busy markets each week and four annual fairs on saints' days and we can be sure that Thomas and Eliza and their families would have been there. There were organisations that met there and maybe Thomas and Eliza took an interest in such things as the growing movement for Catholic emancipation. Loughrea

Typical Irish farmers. They have jackets and shoes so are fairly well off.

The West of Ireland

Showing the towns mentioned in the story

MAYO

ROSCOMMON

GALWAY

●Tuam

Carraroe   Knockatogher

Galway ●

Kilmacdough ●

Loughrea

●Gort

The area in
which the Lallys
and the Littles
were living in
1821

CLARE

TIPPERARY

Dromoland ●

Limerick ●

River Shannon

Bruff○

LIMERICK

KERRY

0   50 miles

© 2022 Stephen Lally and B M Willett

11

boasted a large variety of quite substantial buildings; a town hall, a court-house and prison, a police station and barracks and an army barracks. In the centre was a market hall but Pigot's Directory of 1824 described it as being *'in a wretched state of neglect and decay'*. Loughrea was one of very few towns to have a dispensary or clinic, although the nearest hospital was in Galway city, twenty miles (13km) away. There were twenty public houses listed in Pigot's Directory and about sixty retailers including haberdashers, drapers, ironmongers, boot makers and even a clockmaker. There were three hotels. Loughrea's industry consisted of bakers, soap and candle makers, coachbuilders and farm machinery repairers. In 1821 a new Church of Ireland church was built.

All this was disproportionate to the size of the town's population because these businesses served the countryside for many miles around. Loughrea was a stopover for travellers and they and the police and soldiers stationed there, who would have been almost exclusively Protestant, gave the town a feel that was different from other, smaller towns nearby which were part of simple agricultural and labouring communities. On one hand, Loughrea had 'Society' but if you ventured off the main street, only parts of which were paved, you would have been in a different world of poor, run-down

Typical Irish folk. The farmers have horses and a cart but the woman has no shoes, which was quite normal.   *Illustrated London News*

mud brick houses on streets which, in the frequent wet weather, would have been deep mud. None of Loughrea had mains water or drainage.

Loughrea, like most of Ireland, was in decline at this time. Industry had declined to almost nothing and agricultural prices had collapsed. As a centre of the linen trade, Loughrea had prospered in the 1700s but that had almost disappeared by 1820.

The town's other problem was neglect by the principal landowner. The previous Earl of Clanricarde and his wife had taken some interest in their town and lands but he died in 1808 and his 6 year old son inherited the estate. He seldom visited Ireland and his tenants were in the hands of an agent who was, perhaps, more interested in feathering his own nest than spending money on maintenance, let alone improvements.

Let's now look at the Little and Lally families in detail so we know the childhood backgrounds of Thomas and Eliza. By great good fortune both families are recorded in rare surviving fragments of the 1821 census. They lived two miles apart, in the countryside to the north-west of Loughrea. These census facts are full of clues to our wider story. Some are shown on the family tree charts but they need to be explained in detail in order to set the scene and explain how the Lallys and Littles were related. Our Little and Lally families were related because their mothers were sisters so Thomas and Eliza were first cousins.

The Little family lived in Carraroe, in the parish of Lickerrig. Robert Little, Thomas' father, was the head of the household. His wife was not there on the day of the census and Robert may have been a widower. He described himself as a farmer, nurseryman and gardener with 18 acres. There were thirteen people in the house on the night of the census, nine of them adults of working age, four visitors including Eliza Lally, and a servant called Mary Brett. They are all shown on the chart on page 15.

There were only three houses in Carraroe. Carraroe House was a mansion occupied by William Phibbs Irwin who described himself as a 'Gentleman and Farmer' in the census. He had a wife and at least one son but they must have been elsewhere when the census was taken. He leased two other parcels of land elsewhere, bringing his land to a total of 112 acres. Carraroe House was situated on a hillside which suggests that this was not typical marshy land but was good fertile farmland. To look after the family were five servants, including a groom and a ploughman, indicating he owned horses and ploughs. William Phibbs Irwin was a wealthy man – by Irish standards.

Next to this mansion, or maybe even attached to it, was the house of the Little family. It was a large stone built house, probably a single storey house, but large enough to sleep thirteen people and in the top ten percent of all dwellings in Ireland. It was far better quality than the average Irish house and ruins of these two large houses still exist on this site two hundred years later. Robert Little rented a landholding of 18 acres of good land and this meant that he was comfortably off. Robert's four sons of working age, 21 to 14 years, did not give their occupation but it is likely that they worked on the land at Carraroe House and did not want to put down 'labourer' as it would have reflected badly on the well-to-do image their family would have tried to portray. Robert Little had four visitors; the Kellys and Elizabeth Lally, as she was named in the census, but certainly our Eliza. Later, in Australia, her house was often full of visitors, obviously something they had grown up with in these friendly times at home in Ireland.

Then there was Mary Brett, age 16, the house servant. If Robert had no wife and a large house and family to maintain, he would need a servant if he could afford one. A Brett family lived just across the fields, in what was probably the nearest house to the Littles. There was not much employment for a 16 year old girl so in order to get out of the house and be grown up, as any 16 year old girl would want, she may well have taken this job for not much more than board and lodging. She was almost certainly related but was recorded as a servant.

But there is more to the Bretts. On 27th May 1798 a Robert Little had married a Judith Brett who was living very close to Carraroe and these two were surely Thomas' parents. The names fit and the fact that Thomas, their eldest son, was born 18 months after the marriage fits this assumption. Little and Brett are uncommon surnames in that area, even less common than Lally. Eliza's mother was Annie Lally, née Brett. All these people were living, marrying, staying with each other, all within a couple of miles of each other as was normal in Ireland. It is almost certain that Judith Little and

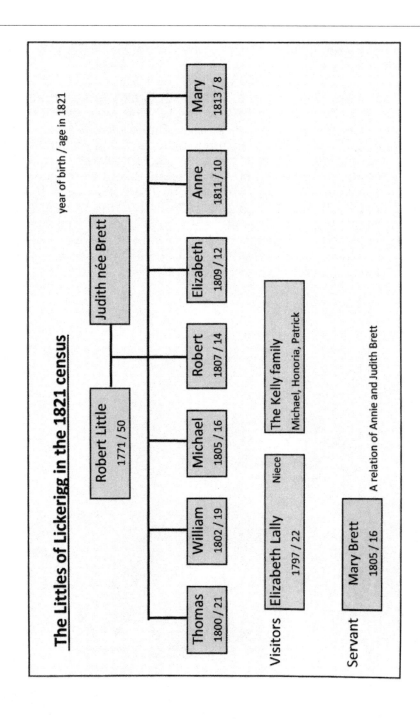

The Littles of Lickerigg in the 1821 census

year of birth / age in 1821

Robert Little 1771 / 50 — Judith née Brett

Thomas 1800 / 21
William 1802 / 19
Michael 1805 / 16
Robert 1807 / 14
Elizabeth 1809 / 12
Anne 1811 / 10
Mary 1813 / 8

Visitors

Elizabeth Lally 1797 / 22 — Niece

The Kelly family — Michael, Honoria, Patrick

Servant

Mary Brett 1805 / 16 — A relation of Annie and Judith Brett

Annie Lally were sisters. That is why Eliza Lally was shown on the census as Robert Little's niece.

There is more. Robert Little and Judith Brett were married in the Church of Ireland church in Loughrea. This was the Protestant church. The Bretts and Lallys were Catholics but this marriage shows that Robert Little was not. Little is not a traditional Irish, Catholic surname. It is common in Protestant Ulster but not in the south of Ireland so it could be that their ancestors were incomers to County Galway. This may explain why the Littles were better off than most Irish as they didn't suffer from the political, legal, employment and educational restrictions placed on Catholics. Judith would have insisted, under pressure from her priest and family, that their children were brought up as Catholics and Thomas was certainly a fervent Catholic in later life.

These are large, impressive and rare Irish houses. One may imagine the one in the foreground being occupied by Phibbs Irwin and the one on the right by the Littles.   *Illustrated London News*

There is another connection. The 1798 marriage record shows that Robert Little was from Coole, near Gort. The wife of William Phibbs Irwin was from that area too. These landed families looked after each other and Robert may have obtained his land next to Carraroe House and employment there on recommendation from the owners of Coole Park. If he obtained that employment before he was married, that would have been how he met Judith Brett who lived just across the fields.

Now we look at the Lallys, whose surname derives from a traditional Connaught clan going back to the great Lords of Hymaine in ancient times, centred on Tollendal Castle near Tuam and with lands stretching far south through Eastern Galway.

At the time of the census in 1821 the Lally family, headed by James and his wife Annie, née Brett, were living in the townland of Knockatogher (pronounced 'Nock-a-to'er', the 'gh' being silent), in the parish of Kiltullagh, about six miles north of Loughrea. It was this sort of area that Eliza grew up in although on the day of the census she was staying with her uncle and cousins, the Littles.

Knockatogher was very different to the land in Carraroe and a complete contrast to the homes and broad landscapes that Eliza would experience later in life. The area consisted of a low, broad hill raised above the surrounding marshland. It wasn't a village but a scattering of shacks and poor houses across an area of about a square mile (2½ sq km). The land was undulating with hillocks and dips that hid any view. The narrow lanes that ran through it were sunk below ground level through centuries of use and further hidden by metre high rough stone walls covered with ivy, moss and shrubs so anybody walking in them would have felt hemmed in on all sides. The surfaces of the small fields were at different levels, all up and down as if a giant had been digging in them. There seemed to be no flat area anywhere. They too were surrounded by the low stone walls. The soil was quite fertile and the crops would most likely have been potatoes and flax, maybe some corn, all dug, planted, tended and harvested by hand.

If you stood on one of the hillocks you would see the sun glinting off the bogs in the distance and you may also have been able to see a corn mill and Rafford House, the only larger buildings in the area. On the southern border of Knockatogher ran the old east – west main road on which some carriages and carts would have rumbled past, creating most of the activity. The road went through Kiltullagh itself, the parish centre, which was recognisable as a tiny village with a few houses, another corn mill, a chapel, a single storey thatched beer house and Kiltullagh House, a four storey square mansion.

The overall impression of the area, as with most of the Irish countryside, was stillness and silence. Any sound would have been muffled by the undulating ground and soft earth. Nobody had a clock or watch and life would have revolved around the rising and setting of the sun and the seasons. There were no lights and the pitch black of night would have shown up the heavens and the myriad stars, emphasising the smallness of humanity and its dependence on nature.

The census tells us that the Lallys had six acres of land which was more than most of their neighbours and just a bit more than the five acres that was considered the minimum to support a family. James Lally said he was a farmer / labourer and his wife Annie was a flax spinner so she, and probably the children who worked with the flax, would have brought in some additional income, although less than before as the price of linen had fallen a lot in her lifetime. The older children would have had to work to support themselves and any child, once they could walk, would have been given jobs to do. Childhood as we know it didn't exist.

A report that we shall come to later describes their house. It would most likely have been built of mud bricks and with a mud floor but even this was much better than a typical country hovel. It had two or more rooms with doors and windows and was large enough for seven people to be seated with one spinning flax. There would have been very little furniture, maybe a bed and some stools, no cupboards as they would have had nothing to store. The house next door had wooden internal doors that could be locked so it is likely that the Lally house was similar. It may have had a chimney and fireplace but let us be in no doubt that it was a small, poor, damp dwelling in which to live and bring up a large family.

Looking at the family helps paint the picture and the chart opposite shows Eliza's family based on the 1821 census and other information. Perhaps the most noticeable contrast with the Littles was that only half the Lally family were living there on the day the census recorded them. It is fair to assume that there were three

The Lallys of Kiltullagh in **1821**

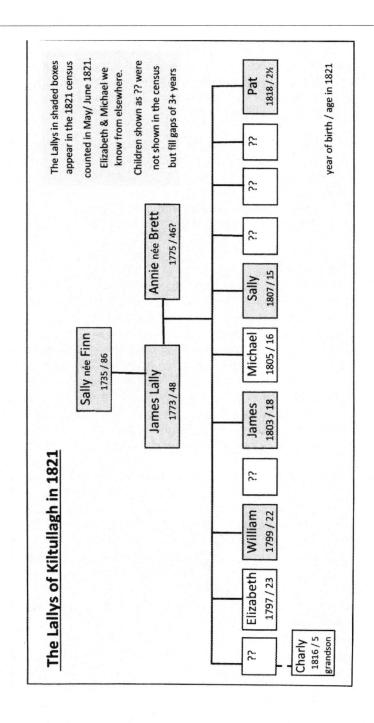

The Lallys in shaded boxes appear in the 1821 census counted in May/ June 1821.

Elizabeth & Michael we know from elsewhere.

Children shown as ?? were not shown in the census but fill gaps of 3+ years

Sally née Finn
1735 / 86

James Lally
1773 / 48

Annie née Brett
1775 / 46?

Elizabeth
1797 / 23

William
1799 / 22

??

James
1803 / 18

Michael
1805 / 16

Sally
1807 / 15

??

??

??

Pat
1818 / 2½

??

Charly
1816 / 5
grandson

year of birth / age in 1821

children in the twelve years between Sally and Pat and they were staying somewhere else. The reason that over half the older children were absent was simply that the house was too small to accommodate them all and the six acres couldn't support them. They'd had to move out to get a job.

It was a typical four generation family. In fact, the youngest child, Pat, was Charly's uncle, yet was younger than his nephew. Eliza (Elizabeth) was more than 21 years older than Pat, but the ages of James and Annie Lally and the presence of their little grandson, Charly Lally, suggest there was a son older than Eliza. Details of Eliza's death, many years hence, tell us she was born in May 1797.

William, the next brother, was described as 'insane' in the census. This was entered in the 'occupation' box, suggesting he was not fit to work. On 10th July 1821, after the family was recorded for the census, he was to commit an act so dreadful that it was reported in the national newspapers and in a report to parliament in London. In a sudden and unprovoked fit of rage, while at home, he attacked his sister Sally and, when his grandmother intervened, he killed her with an iron spade, chopping her head off with it. He then proceeded to do the same to an elderly neighbour. William was tried and found guilty of murder so presumably hanged. This must have had a dramatic effect on the whole family. They moved away and no more is known for certain of Eliza's family after this but it was the newspaper reports that gave the useful description of their house.

It is most likely that there was another child in the four years between William and James. He or she may have died. Nothing is known of James Lally, born in 1803, other than the details in the census which show him as a labourer. We know of Michael, who was born in 1805, as he features in our story as he went with Thomas and Eliza to India. In 1823 he records his occupation as 'clerk' which suggests he was educated, a fact which seems to conflict with the image of the family as poorer members of the community and may suggest a side to them that we cannot see. They were not just poor peasants. Then there was Sally who was listed in the census and was the initial subject of her brother's murderous rage in the July. From Sally to Pat there is the twelve year gap but the report of the murder says that Sally was looking after four young brothers and sisters so these three extra children are included in our tree as blank spaces. It was quite common for people, especially children to move freely between different parts of the family, as demonstrated by Eliza. Any child over the age of 12, and maybe younger, would have been in work and could have been away at this location or lodging with family nearby. They all mixed in together and the standard of accommodation was not what we may imagine today. Many homes had only one room where everybody ate and slept and it was not unusual for workers to all sleep together in a rough, leaking shack.

Little Pat needs a special mention as it is he who started this whole historical saga. Patrick is your writer's great great grandfather who went to London, probably in the early 1840s. He most likely had a job in Ireland as a nurseryman and gardener as this was always his occupation in London. This was the same occupation as Thomas and Robert Little. Patrick married in London and had nine children, eight of whom survived to adulthood. He had responsible jobs and his best times were when he owned a mushroom nursery in Kensington, supplying big houses and smart restaurants in London. But he fell on hard times, perhaps through drink and gambling or by the new Metropolitan underground railway destroying his nursery.

The Lally family's house may have been like this. It has a door, windows, roof and chimney so was comfortable by Irish standards. ILN.

The last fifteen years of his life were spent in the workhouse or Catholic institutions but the big story he told in later life was of what might have been. He told various tales of how he could have been rich in the wine business in Swan River, Western Australia. What he meant only became apparent when it was discovered that it was his sister, Eliza, who went to Swan River. So little Pat is responsible for this book, from the 1821 census when he was 2½ years old to us now knowing the ending.

Many thousands of Irish people emigrated every year and it seems that our Lally family from a small house among the bogs of Galway followed their example. Eliza and Thomas would have seen relations emigrate to England, and most likely to America too. Venturing into the realms of conjecture, there is a strong DNA link between your writer and a family in America whose ancestry goes back to a Thomas Lally from Kiltullagh who emigrated to Massachusetts. His age suggests he could have been our James Lally Senior's brother but, as well as Thomas Lally, that American family's ancestors include other younger Lallys, including one who married in Galway in 1831 before emigrating. There were several Lally families around Milford, Massachusetts, from the same area of Galway and they could have been Eliza's relatives. The strong DNA link and the link to Kiltullagh show that these emigrants to America were cousins or brothers and sisters of our Lally family in the Kiltullagh area. It remains a mystery now, but more information may emerge in the future that will reveal a whole new chapter of the family story. It is most likely that relatives of Eliza had already emigrated and set an example to her and the Littles. Emigration was commonplace.

Both our families, the Littles and Lallys faced disruption after 1821. It was not surprising that the Lally family moved away from Kiltullagh after the murders. Most young Lally men were already working away from home at the time of the census and this was quite normal. They couldn't all survive on just six acres. In 1823 Michael Lally, who is important to our story, was a clerk at Bruff in County Limerick, 65 miles due south of Loughrea. Work was hard to come by and if you had any ambition beyond subsistence farming you had to move away.

The Littles at Carraroe seem to have been split up at this time too. William Phibbs-Irwin died in December 1822 and the lease of Carraroe House was taken up by one of his brothers in law, John

Dennis. The rental of the various pieces of land changed then and it is likely that John Dennis took over the 18 acres that had been farmed by the Littles.

Two other brothers of Thomas Little are important to our story; William and Robert Jr. Both of them soon had jobs as labourers in a vast new mansion being constructed from 1822 at Dromoland, 35 miles (56km) south of Loughrea and midway to Bruff. This was the largest construction project in Ireland at that time and was to be the new home of the Barons of Inchiquin. The grand house was to be set in 1500 acres of landscaped grounds at the confluence of the Rivers Shannon and Fergus. When completed in 1835 it was said to be the most beautiful house in Ireland. Many skilled craftsmen were employed in this work but both William and Robert claimed only to be labourers which meant they were poorly paid and probably lived in very rough communal accommodation.

Dromoland Castle, depicted here in 1840, was completed in 1835 so William and Robert Jr. would never have seen it like this. Compare this building, with its sweeping grounds and magnificent interior, with the humble dwellings of most Irishmen. Today it is a 5 star hotel. Taken from the book "A Series of Picturesque Views of the Seats of Noblemen and Gentlemen of Great Britain and Ireland" by Francis Orpen Morris.

IRELAND

CHAPTER 2

THOMAS' AND ELIZA'S IRELAND

Now we know the Little and Lally families we can now look more broadly at what life was like for them in the first twenty years of the nineteenth century. And we should start with the background to Irish history, even if it means condensing several centuries into a few paragraphs. It's easy to look at historical events as if they occurred in quick succession because in a readable book that's how they follow one another. But the shape of Irish society, the background that so affected the lives of our families had developed over many decades and generations and it is difficult to change the course of such momentum without drastic action. In the end it was drastic action that our families, the Littles and the Lallys, had to take and that is the theme of this story.

The Battle of the Boyne in 1690 was a turning point in Irish history. To put it bluntly, the Catholics lost and the Protestants won. New punitive laws were introduced to suppress Catholicism. No Catholic was permitted any but the most menial job in the government, police, military or education. Catholics were not allowed to build churches. Land was confiscated from the major Catholic protagonists of 1690 and given to Protestants. No Catholic was permitted to buy land and, by law, Catholic land had to be divided equally between sons at death. So, for example, a Catholic man with 100 acres and five sons had to give 20 acres to each of his sons. On death, if each of those sons had their own five sons, each would receive an impractical four acres. Within just a few generations Catholic land-owning was all but wiped out. Yet in 1801 over 90% of the population was Catholic.

Most of these penal laws had been removed by the end of the 18th century and the Act of Union of 1801 made Ireland an integral part of the United Kingdom in a futile attempt to treat Ireland exactly the same as the rest of Britain. These repeals benefitted all Catholics throughout Britain but they affected Ireland most. However, Ireland had many problems of its own that compounded the woes of the Irish peasantry, a major one being that of absentee landlords. The owners of many big estates in Ireland had large houses in England too. Why would they wish to live in Ireland, remote from society, with its uneconomic, depressed agriculture and surrounded by antagonistic peasants. There was none of the paternalism so often found on English estates where all levels of society had lived with and depended on each other for generations. Absentee landlords usually left the collecting of rent from tenants to agents whose sole motivation was collecting as much money as possible. They, in turn, often passed this responsibility down and down to sub-agents so that as many as eight people lived by passing rent from the peasant to the ultimate landowner with the result that nobody cared. Tenants could be evicted at will so nobody improved their land because they had no future on it and improvement would only result in the rent being raised. Vast areas of land were barely usable. Large amounts of agricultural products were exported to England where they achieved better prices and the profit was not invested back in Ireland. Even many local landlords were penniless as their land was unsaleable and worthless.

Despite all this, there were some good years for agriculture leading to an explosion in the population which doubled between 1780 and 1820. Ireland was the most densely populated country in Europe and visitors said it also had the worst poverty.

Whereas nearly every stream in the north of England had a mill or factory driven by it, the industrial revolution had not reached Ireland. Prices of manufactured goods fell in the early 1800s destroying many a small Irish factory in the process. A principal Irish export was linen and many families survived by growing flax for its manufacture. But in these years the vast mills of the north of England could produce linen and sell it cheaper in Loughrea than it could be produced locally. Falling back on dependence on agriculture was no help when free trade was introduced in 1815 and grain prices plummeted. The population was driven more and more to subsistence dependence on the potato. The potato is very nutritious, as good as the English labourer's bread and cheese, and it produces five times the nutrition from one acre than do grains. But by the 1820s in Connaught, 70% of the population only ate potatoes and 80% of all food eaten was potato. Such dependence on a crop that was prone to disease and didn't store from one year to the next was extremely precarious.

As English agriculture became more efficient any surplus labour moved to the new factories and new towns. There were neither in Ireland so where could the children of large families go if their father's five acres could not support them? Many eked out a meagre existence on hillsides in appalling conditions, under hedges or in huts made of sticks and mud. The only way to increase the efficiency of agriculture was to increase the size of plots and this led to the dreadful evictions of families and whole villages, the occupants of which had nowhere to go.

Despite the 1841 census being twenty years ahead of our story it offers the best survey of Irish housing. The census returns split housing into four categories, the worst being a mud cabin with no windows or chimney. It stated that 52% of the population lived in this condition. Yet several priests in Connaught declared that the census missed all the population out on the hillsides in even worse conditions. One priest repeated the census himself and added another third to the population of his parish, that extra third living in conditions even worse than a mud cabin with no windows or chimney.

Typical dwellings of half of the Irish people.   *Illustrated London News*

Legally suppressed, industry destroyed, dependence on one food staple, appalling living conditions and nowhere else to go; it was a disaster waiting to happen. Around the turn of that century it was estimated that a localised famine occurred every three years, caused by potato blight or rot in sodden fields. It was particularly bad in 1800, 1807 and 1816-17. Disaster struck the west of Ireland, where our families lived, in 1821 and 1822 when a very wet season destroyed nearly all the crop. Such was the rain that many mud houses were just washed away. The government estimated that a million people were living on the edge of starvation. In fact, many did die of starvation and of typhus.

There were two societies in Ireland. Not only were there Catholics and Protestants but the two societies spoke different languages. Many Gaelic speaking poor would probably only know enough English to take instructions from their employer, if they had one. Eliza's family would have spoken Gaelic as their first language, but also probably knew some English so that they could communicate with Thomas' family who probably spoke mostly English. The very poor, who formed the vast majority, lived from hand to mouth and by barter and prayed that the Good Lord would provide for them that day. They had little need of the coins used by the traders in Loughrea. They had one set of scanty clothes that they wore day and night and many never possessed shoes. The Littles were comfortably above this level. When disaster struck the Lallys could afford to move away, thus demonstrating that even they were better off than most.

These are the sort of dwellings ignored in the 1841 census. Perhaps a third of Irish people lived like this.   *Illustrated London News*

The year 1821 was a key year in our story. There is much detail of our families in the census in the middle of that year. This was followed by the dreadful murders in July. By September 1821 the whole area would have known that they were to be gripped by a severe famine in 1822 because, as the potatoes were harvested it was obvious that most of the crop was rotten. The weather had been exceptionally wet all year. The population in large areas was to be reduced to surviving on nettles, roots and seaweed for two years and thousands died of starvation or typhus that preyed on the malnourished. A large relief programme was set up but handouts were usually given in return for work on public projects such as roads, bridges and marsh draining. It is likely that our Littles and Lallys, as clerks, gardeners and labourers working for the section of society that had enough money, survived this better than most but the famine led to greatly increased protest among rural groups such as the Ribbonmen who committed a number of outrages in East Galway. A mile from the home of the Littles was Dunsandle, the home of Lord Dunsandle, the Lallys' and Littles' landlord. His grounds, gardens and nurseries extended to a square mile and may have been where Thomas Little was employed as gardener. But Lord Dunsandle was a harsh and unpopular landlord, notorious for his suppression of any protest and, in 1822, for his conviction and hanging of Ribbonmen. Our families were probably a bit to the east of the worst famine areas but were in the thick of the protests and would certainly have had an opinion on these matters.

The reasons why our families and so many others felt they had to leave Ireland in order to better themselves are becoming clear. Things were getting worse, generation by generation, and Thomas and Eliza probably saw this in their own families. Previous generations of Thomas' family, in particular, seem to have had much better times compared with the menial jobs he and his brothers now had in their youth. There were key events in their formative years that must have convinced them that things were not going to get better; the collapse of prices of manufactured goods, including linen, free trade in 1815 which destroyed markets for agricultural goods, frequent localised famines, including bad ones locally in 1821 and 1822, suppression of protest. What would become of their children if things continued to get worse? The probable loss of the Little's family home at Carraroe may have been a personal trigger to making a brave change.

Reading this, you must be asking if there were any redeeming features to life in Ireland at this time. Remarkably, people travelling through Ireland reported that the people themselves maintained their cheerful Irish disposition. They thanked God for what they had, they celebrated the many saints' days with a fiddle player and some poteen and were always generous to strangers and those worse off than themselves. This was the only life they knew, although they had heard back from those who had already left for better lives in foreign lands. There was little to do between planting and harvesting potatoes so there was plenty of time for talking, singing and dancing, and always a reason for a celebration.

IRELAND

CHAPTER 3

TO A NEW LIFE

It is very likely that the two families who had grown up so closely together and who had now been forced apart in the search for work all came home for the great celebration of the marriage of Thomas Little and Eliza Lally – the childhood sweethearts.

Neither Thomas, at the age of 22 or 23, nor Eliza, at about 25, were young for a couple getting married in Ireland at that time. They were first cousins. Such marriages were not uncommon in these close communities but this may have been a cause of hesitancy. From 1835 permission for such a marriage had to be granted by the bishop. It's likely that when Thomas decided that he had to leave Ireland he was confronted by the fact that he could not bring himself to leave Eliza behind and they couldn't go together unless they were married. Whatever the details, it was a marriage worth fighting for. Unfortunately, no record survives of the place or date of the wedding but it took place at some time between the census in mid 1821 and Thomas signing up for the army in May 1823.

Many weddings took place in the homes of the bride or groom and not in church, but what a wedding it must have been. With so many young Irish people, weddings were frequent but always the best reason for a big celebration. This was a wedding that everybody knew was coming – one day. Now it was here, and, along with the solemnity of the ceremony, came so many Irish traditions; the rich fruit cake, the mead, the ritual binding of the couple's hands and, of course, the music, singing and dancing, led by the bride and groom. It would have been a grand family reunion with up to four generations making a happy day of it. Of course, so many children would have been at the front taking it all in, including Eliza's youngest brother, Pat, who would have been only 4 or 5 years old.

But it must have been a bitter-sweet occasion. The beautiful young couple, so optimistic and impetuous. The celebrations going on in the knowledge that they would soon leave their home, families and friends, probably never to be seen again.

A recurring theme in this story will be the search for reasons why Thomas and Eliza, and their brothers, were successful in later life, so just as we imagined those questions about his auspicious birth date being asked at Thomas' baptism, we now ask the question; Can a man's choice of wife affect his life? With more certainty, we can answer, "Yes". Eliza, being 2½ years older than Thomas, must have tried to mother him as a baby. They could have grown up more as brother and sister, as partners and equals. As they grew, they would have shared joys, sorrows and ambitions long before they formally joined hands on life's journey. As adults Eliza is likely to have been a mature support and valued adviser rather than a submissive and subservient companion as were so many wives in those days. Eliza was to play a large part in Thomas' success.

The young men of our families wondered what future they had in Ireland. They decided they had to leave, so in May 1823 William and Thomas Little and Michael Lally enlisted in the Army of the Honourable East India Company. Michael Lally enlisted (or attested) first, on 8th May in Dublin, followed by William Little on 16th in Cork and Thomas Little on 22nd in Dublin. Five weeks later, on 1st July, Robert Little enlisted in Dublin. Had they all decided to join and signed up when it was convenient or did Michael kick it off and one by one they joined him? It would seem that Robert, the youngest to go, may have needed some encouragement. They all joined the Artillery and all joined to go to The Bengal Presidency. Michael Little, James Lally and any other adult brothers decided to stay. 19th July 1823 was the big day when Thomas, William and Robert joined their Battalion together in Dublin. Michael Lally, although he was the first to enlist, joined them on 9th August.

With them on 19th July was Matthias Glynn who plays a part in our story. He was a gardener from Kilmacdough, right on the southern border of Co. Galway, about 18 miles from Loughrea. He signed up in Cork in mid June. No family connection can be found so either he was a friend or they met in Dublin and became friends in the army.

In the light of today's, perhaps simplistic, impressions of Irish history and the antagonism between Catholics and Protestants, Irish and English, it may be considered odd that Irish men, and Catholics too, were joining a British Army. But there were many, often contradictory, sides to Irish opinion and many an Irishman had a pride in the Empire and wanted to be included in its success. And this wasn't His Majesty's British Army. It was the army of the Honourable East India Company, frequently just known as The Company, and Catholics were allowed join too.

They signed up because they saw no future for themselves in Ireland. If they wished to emigrate, then England, Canada or America were the choices at that time but they had to pay the fare. The Company Army offered emigration free of charge. The Army offered a job for life, security and structure, compared with the unemployment and poverty wages at home. The Army offered free food and accommodation for life. It offered a glamorous uniform. Of course, there was also the recruiting sergeant who was paid according to the number of recruits he enrolled. He regaled men with tales of adventure in exotic lands, a utopian escape from all of Ireland's problems.

The Company Army was in competition with His Majesty's Army for recruits and they were facing a severe shortage. In 1820 they had managed to recruit only 1,354 men in the whole of Britain, against a target of 4,009 so the following years saw a push in Ireland. In 1820 The Company had set up a permanent recruitment office in Dublin and then another in Cork in 1822 but records show that recruiting sergeants travelled to towns all over Ireland. An analysis of 519 East India Company Artillery Recruits who joined at about the same time as Our Family, 1822-4, shows that 59% were Irish and most of them would have been Catholics.

From now on, for brevity, we shall refer to the Honourable East India Company as 'The Company' and to Thomas and Eliza, and William, Robert Jr. and Michael as 'Our Family'.

Why did Our Family join The Company Army, rather than the British Army? The British Army had troops in Ireland who marched through towns with grand parades which successfully enticed recruits. The Company Army could not do that because their troops were in India but a major enticement was the pension. Our Family all signed up for life, which meant eighteen years. After that they would receive a pension of nine pence a day for the rest of their lives. That would be a fortune if they stayed in India and a good income if they opted for free travel home to Ireland. The fact that fewer than 10% of men lived long enough in India to claim that pension was probably not explained to them.

Another advantage of the Company Army was that you knew where you were going – India, one of the most glorious parts of the British Empire. In the British Army you could be posted anywhere in the world at very short notice and, if you had a wife and family, they would most likely be left behind, alone for years – an unknown number of years. Then there was the bounty. The British Army paid you £3/4/0 (£3.20) when you joined. It was a large amount and they bought you with it. The Company Army paid more and if Thomas, William and Robert each had given half to their father, as many often did, that would be a year's wages for him. It was a big inducement to men who were poor, may have been hungry and had grave doubts about their future. It was a tangible demonstration of the Recruiting Sergeant's blarney about the wonderful, secure, even prosperous future that lay ahead for them. And, of course, they were all young, adventurous and oblivious of the risks.

Many men signed up to The Company Army or British Army on the spur of the moment; the glamour of the big parade, the secure future and bounty. It seems, however, that for Our Family it was a considered decision. They each travelled long distances to sign up in different places at about the same time, so it wasn't a sudden, impulse decision in their home town. They had discussed it.

Our Family were to stick together through thick and thin – and what a family they were. They had all managed to join the Artillery which was a much smaller force than the Infantry. It may be too much to call the Artillery an elite force but certainly only a better quality of men in terms of health and physique were accepted and they were to be looked up to. Our four men certainly exceeded these criteria. When they met together in the army in Dublin, on the ship out and in their barracks in Calcutta they turned heads wherever they went. The Littles were giants, an irony that cannot have gone un-noticed by their fellow soldiers. The Register of Recruits into The Company Army is available today, giving many personal details. The study of

519 Artillery recruits and of 456 Infantry recruits in 1822-4 proves that our men were exceptional.

The minimum permitted height of an Artillery recruit was 5'6" (1.68m) and this was strictly adhered to. The average height of Artillery recruits was 5' 7½" (1.72m) and two thirds of them were 5'6" or 5'7" (1.68m or 1.70m). William Little was 6' 1¼" (1.86m). Among the 519, there were only two soldiers taller than him – and by less than an inch. He was in the top 1% in terms of height. Thomas was 5' 11¾" (1.83m) and in the top 2%. Robert was 5' 9¼" (1.76m) and even he was in the top 10%. And Artillery recruits were taller than Infantry.

The minimum permitted height of an Infantry recruit was 5'5" (1.65m) but this was clearly not adhered to. 70% of Infantry recruits were between 5'5" and 5'6". But of these, 60% were exactly 5'5" a consistency that is not believable in the population as a whole. Infantry recruitment was "flexible". For example, if a man was classed as "a growing lad" he could be admitted at under 5'5", yet none of the recruits were under 19 years old so unlikely to still be growing. Also there was desperate need for high recruit numbers and a good bonus for every recruit for the Recruiting Sergeant. It has to be that a great proportion of Infantry recruits recorded as 5'5" were shorter than this.

It was for the Artillery that taller and stronger men were demanded and even among the Artillery, the Littles were the tallest. In the general population there must have been many men below 5'4" and women even shorter. Adults under 5'0" (1.52m) were not unusual in Ireland so the Littles must have towered above them and be considered giants. Even Michael Lally, at 5'7¼" (1.71m), was well above the average of the general population. Looking at the three main military protagonists of the previous decade, shows Admiral Nelson at 5'4" (1.63m), Napoleon at 5'6" (1.68m) and the US President, James Madison at 5'4" (1.63m)

Can a man's height affect his life? Tall men are looked up to in more ways than one. Height can give a man confidence and authority, enabling him to push his promotion prospects. Their distinctive height made them stand out from the crowd, particularly when they were together. It could easily have been a factor in their subsequent success and is it too farfetched to wonder if the 'Little' name helped by accentuating their height and stature?

Men of the Bengal Foot Artillery proudly wear their uniforms, the tall caps making them appear even taller. Painted in 1845 by Henry Martens, they are very similar to how Our Family would have looked. © Anne S.K. Brown Military Collection at victorianweb.org

Michael Lally, Eliza's brother, stood out for another reason. He was average height but had red hair and blue/grey eyes. Hair colours were generally recorded in many shades of brown, including 'sandy' that we might call ginger. But Michael's hair was red, suggesting a distinctive bright red. Fewer than one in a hundred recruits had red hair. What a shame that we don't have the same details for Eliza. Was she a fiery red-haired beauty? It is so difficult to imagine old people when they were young and full of enthusiasm, optimism and zest for life.

Eliza had to be signed up too as the number of soldiers who could take wives with them was strictly limited. Depending on regiment it was between 5% and 8%. Wives were considered a complication and an unnecessary distraction from military single-mindedness and discipline. She had to commit to military discipline; to do what she was told, to carry out tasks such as cleaning or cooking in order to earn her keep and to curtsey to senior officers as a soldier would salute.

There is a time in life when you stay in a rut or gamble everything on a better future and for Our Family, there was no going back. They all signed up for life. Their bounty had bought them and desertion, if it would ever occur to them, brought harsh penalties of jail, corporal punishment or deportation. They could never go home because that would be the first place the military would look. Like emigrants of all types, they accepted that, whatever happened, it was very unlikely they would ever see their home and families again, a concept incomprehensible today with aircraft, photography and the internet. Even return correspondence by letter could take a year from India.

The five had changed their lives for ever in the hope of a brighter future of adventure, opportunity and security. They didn't know then that only two of them would see their 30th birthday.

INDIA

CHAPTER 4

THE VOYAGE

They had left home - for ever. The new recruits would have sailed out of Dublin within a few weeks of joining The Company Army, so probably by the end of August 1823. Some may never have seen a sea-going ship before and it would have been their first experience of being on board a ship at sea. The journey from Dublin, round the south coast of Britain and into the Thames estuary would have taken about two weeks, depending on the weather, and it would not have been a happy time. Most of them would have been sea-sick. On arrival, their new, temporary home was Chatham Barracks, about 30 miles (50km) east of the City of London and its great port and in one of the main military areas of Britain.

Chatham Army Barracks was an appalling place used by His Majesty's troops as well as The Company's. It was in separate buildings outside Chatham Naval Dockyard. It had been built in 1757 so was 65 years old by the time Our Family arrived there and had not been well cared for. Living conditions were cramped and appalling, even by the standards of the time with poor cooking, washing and sanitary facilities. There was no separate mess hall. By now Eliza would have got used to the fact that wives shared all the accommodation and facilities with hundreds of men with perhaps only a sheet rigged up to give a little privacy. This was considered acceptable because it was said that the life of the poor included much communal living, but this was not a fair comparison because it was within the family – not with fifty men crammed in an open-plan barrack room. A Royal Commission of 1857, 33 years later, described conditions at Chatham which would have applied just as much in 1820s. Conditions for wives among so many coarse men with their foul language, antics and nudity were described as degrading in the extreme and a national disgrace. The situation was not helped by the fact that discipline was totally rigid to instill the military regime into young men who had seldom been subject to much control and many would have found this extremely hard and stressful. Much of the men's time was taken up in parades and instruction and there was very little space or provision for off-duty recreation. For young Eliza to be among this crowd of rough and boisterous young men when they had nothing to do must have been frightening, embarrassing and degrading. The women's situation was not helped by many a Sergeant Major who believed that the army was no place for women and any indignities they suffered were entirely their own fault for being there. The women would have had to stick together and Thomas must have been forced to act verbally and physically at times to protect her. Even Eliza herself must have soon learnt to slap a young man down when he overstepped the mark. The image this conjures up is very different from that obtained from the photograph of the kindly old gentleman in his later years. Both Thomas and Eliza had a tough side to them.

The situation cannot have improved when they boarded the cramped ship which was to take them to their new lives in India. Their ship was *Macqueen* and she had spent a few weeks being unloaded in Blackwall Dock in the centre of London after returning from her maiden voyage to India and China. While this was happening a new crew was recruited and goods loaded for her next voyage. Her new cargo included lead, cable, chain, copper and 8 tons of chalk, and a considerable amount of wood was loaded to build billets to convert the ship to a troop carrier. On 15th December 1823 *Macqueen* had been towed out into the Thames by two of the new steam packet boats, *Eclipse* and *Venus*, and taken the 25 miles down stream to Gravesend. Steam ships had only been introduced to the Thames in 1815 and were still a great novelty. Although *Eclipse* and *Venus* were designed for passengers, their use in pulling big sailing ships out into the main stream was being taken advantage of as, with them, this journey would take only a day instead of several days depending on wind and tide and with a pilot on board.

Macqueen was an East Indiaman, built locally in 1821 and she was one of the largest ships in the East India Company fleet, being 1,333 tons, with a gross length of 166 (50m) and gross width of 43 feet (13m). At just over double the marked-out length of a modern tennis court she was very large for that time.

Compare Macqueen, at 1,333 tons with the largest modern ships:
The Queen Elizabeth aircraft carrier, commissioned in 2015 and the pride of the British navy is 65,000 tons.
The Ever Given container ship which got stuck in the Suez Canal in 2021 is 200,000 tons.

East Indiamen owned by The Company were a distinctive brown colour with broad white stripe and built for maximum cargo, rather than speed. They were distinctive in that they were cargo ships, passenger and troop ships and men-o-war.

They were armed for a reason which was that they were open to attack and capture by French or American ships or pirates. By 1824 the threat from the French and Americans had disappeared but pirates could still be a problem. As late as 1831 an India bound ship, *Guildford*, was lost at sea with all hands, presumably going

Venus, Built in 1821, she was one of the two steam ships that towed Macqueen out into the Thames estuary. This 1823 etching shows her entering the harbour at Margate. The sailing boats show clearly that Venus was heading into strong wind. Artist was W L Huggins. (Margate History)

down in tropical storm. Yet a few years later it was reported that an English woman, Ann Presgrave, had been sold to a Malay chief. Ann was a passenger on *Guildford*, indicating that she had, in fact, been taken by pirates.

In Gravesend more cargo was put on board and also the guns and powder. The crew was on board and they included twelve Marine Society boys. These boys were orphans who had been schooled to have a life at sea. They were between the ages of 12 and 14 and this was to be their first voyage.

By the beginning of January 1824 victualling had started; the loading of salted pork and beef, grains and other dry supplies, beer and rum for the crew. It took several days to fill the fresh water tanks as it

Repulse

An East Indiaman of exactly the same size as Macqueen. She is shown here in 1839 in East India Dock Basin. Artist was Charles Henry Seaforth. (National Maritime Museum, London)

must be remembered that everything was loaded and stored by hand. On 13th January fresh supplies were loaded and these consisted of live animals for meat and eggs. Exactly what was loaded on *Macqueen* is not detailed but a good idea can be obtained from the list of animals loaded on the Company ship, *Marchioness of Ely* in June 1822. This was recorded in a Journal written by John Luard, a junior officer on board. He went on to have an illustrious career in the Army and as an artist, several of his paintings illustrating this story. *Marchioness of Ely* was 30% smaller than *Macqueen* but still took on board 528 ducks and hens, 56 pigs and 70 sheep. None of these would survive the journey but the ship's company ate reasonably well. Horses were loaded on *Macqueen* too. These were not for food but for military use in India. On 14th and 15th January the paying passengers boarded. On Thursday morning, 15th January 1824 the 200 soldiers marched the 10 miles from Chatham through the sleet and at 1pm boarded their home for the next 135 days. Thomas, William and Robert Little are each recorded. Michael Lally is there and Mathias Glynn who we will hear more of later. '*Eliza, wife of Thos Little*' was also logged on board.

Marchioness of Ely is shown here in front of General Hewitt. She was drawn on 16th June 1822 by John Luard. This is the ship that was 30% smaller than Macqueen yet took on board all the livestock listed above. (Royal Museums, Greenwich, London)

The ship's log provides all this detail, and a great deal more, and it is included here to set the scene for their voyage. All this on a ship the length of two tennis courts, but what must be added is detail of the human cargo. There was a total of 375 souls on board, as well as all that cargo, the supplies and food animals and the horses. Everyone was listed by name.

The Commander was James Walker. His Officers were Chief Mate and second to sixth Mates, Surgeon, Boatswain, Purser, Gunner, Carpenter, six Midshipmen, Caulker to keep the ship watertight and a Cooper to look after the barrels of fresh water. There was a sail maker, Captain's and ship's cooks, a poulterer to look after all the chickens and a butcher to despatch them and the other animals. A total of 26 senior men. The senior officers had servants and many others had Mates, or seconds in command, adding another 21 men. Crew consisted of 41 seamen, 28 ordinary seamen, 19 landsmen and the 12 Marine Boys; a total of 100 exactly.

Paying passengers consisted of a Captain in the Company's Native Infantry, an Ensign, a junior officer, and his wife and a River Pilot. There were four 'Writers', the most junior rank in the Indian Civil Service. There were twelve 'Cadets', the rank held by those who expected to join the Officers in The Company army. All these had to pay their way and could have paid extra to eat at the Commander's table, in other words to get the best food. These added another 20.

Then there were 200 soldier recruits and, listed separately, were 8 wives. The recruits included an Acting Staff Sergeant, seven Acting Sergeants and eight Acting Corporals to keep control. There was a groom recorded as being "in charge of the Honourable Company's Horses during the voyage". Our Family were not among these acting NCOs. This adds 208 to the total.

Of these Officers, their Mates and servants, 47 in all, seven were to die of tropical diseases or drowning before the ship returned to London and five of the 100 crew were to die. This was quite normal. In the one year of 1828 a total of 21 Company Officers lost their lives at sea. This was just the officers who made up a small minority of those on board. But every passenger and recruit survived the first leg of *Macqueen's* journey which was London to Calcutta, Bengal.

The early part of the year was the most frequent time for sailing from England; the sailing season. This gave the best chance of avoiding tropical storms that could tear a ship to pieces. In 1825 another East Indiaman survived a cyclone that took its main mast and most of its rigging. As it limped on it hit uncharted rocks and sank. Also in 1825 *Kent*, carrying soldiers and a cargo of gunpowder caught fire during a storm in the Bay of Biscay. The troop commander was credited with so organising his troops to aid the abandonment before the ship blew up that, of the 629 on board, only 76 lost their lives which was considered a miracle. Fortunately, there had been other ships close at hand. On average, more than one Company ship was lost each year. These dramatic events were recorded in the press in gruesome detail with heroic stories of the survivors. Such tales can only have added to the fears of passengers of all classes as they boarded.

MacQueen sailed on 15th January 1824, gently drifting out into the Thames estuary and unfurling her sails to catch the wind. The soldiers saw very little of this from their quarters just above the water line – 208 of them crammed in there. You couldn't have passengers on deck at such a critical time when all crew were needed for accurate manoeuvring so Our Family would have seen nothing. The creaking, banging and shouting all about the soldiers as they sat in the gloom must have given them time to think of what on earth they had let themselves in for and what the future held. Journeys of this sort were dangerous but most things were dangerous in those days. Staying at home was dangerous and held no opportunity for them. Our Family was together and they were certain that nothing could happen to them and confident in all the opportunities that lay ahead. Or were they? Any confidence and optimism would have been sorely tested by the fear of not being in control, shut in – locked in. This fear would certainly be tested in the next two weeks but then all would be well. It would have to be, as by this time they had no choice.

Macqueen had three decks. At the bottom was the hold. The upper deck held cabins for paying passengers and some of the senior crew. The middle deck was where our soldiers were billeted. It had fourteen portholes and, unusual because of the ship's size, the height of this deck was 6' 4½" (1.94m). Beams would have reduced this height by up to 10", to 5'6½" in places so it was not a comfortable place to walk around in for anybody over 6'. But, typically, in a ship of this sort the headroom was a maximum of 5'8" so the extra height on *Macqueen* was a bonus for our tall family. It is easy to calculate how much space there was for our men. The keel length of Macqueen was 134 feet (43m) and with an internal width of less than 43 feet (13m) it gave each person on the middle deck about 25 sq ft (2.3 sq m). But most of the space was taken up by bunk beds and tables down the middle. With a washing area and toilets taking more space, and with ladders to get on deck and down to the hold, it was very cramped. Two beds in a maximum height of 6' 4½" gave hardly enough room for sitting up in bed. The beds were short too, probably less than the height of all our men. There would have been just enough room to stand between bunks. So our tall family would have had little chance to stretch to their full height unless they lay on the floor.

Several Journals describe the situation on similar Company ships, including the memoir of Sergeant MacMullen who went to India in 1840. His memoir is outlined in '*Following the Drum*'. For him, things were much the same as in Chatham Barracks with the added torture of being crammed in the bottom of a ship. In the opinion of those from poor backgrounds who may have been used to a diet of bread and cheese or potato, the food was good and usually plentiful, with salt meat stew on most days. There was lots of bread with lashings of suet. In bad weather when cooking was difficult the troops had to make do with ship's biscuit, as hard as rock. Water was foul but drinkable because there was nothing else.

He said that with so many bodies down there, the air became "*sickening, foul and repulsive*", not helped by the lanterns which gave the only light but were fuelled by whale oil which, if cheap, gave off a pungent fishy smell. The portholes would be shut most of the time and the only openings to give ventilation were two or three hatches to ascend and descend. To try to maximise air flow the soldiers were not usually allowed to hang sheets round their beds to gain some sort of privacy and, as Sgt MacMullen pointed out, this particularly affected the women. Like so many, MacMullen was outraged by women's conditions among so many men and Eliza was among them. He thought it a gross violation of human decency, the following passage from his memoir showing his feelings.

"The poor women, lowly as their condition was, felt bitterly the indelicacy of their situation. To give them separate sleeping berths would prevent many an immoral and indecent occurrence on shipboard, alike disgraceful to the military service and to human nature. Convicts, if I mistake not, are kept separate and why not the wives of soldiers, allowing none but their husbands or families to occupy the same apartment with them? . . . It is in vain that every soldier is provided with a Bible and Prayer Book . . . if this Spartan indelicacy be forced upon them, the demoralisation of them and the men must follow."

The illustration gives you an idea of the living conditions, come rain or shine, wind or calm, hot or cold, for 135 days. What on earth did they do for all this time?

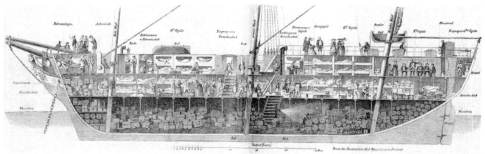

These two illustrations, below decks in steerage and a longitudinal section of a typical emigrant ship, show scenes similar to that on board Macqueen. Illustrated London News

It is fortunate that disease did not get hold of the troops on *Macqueen* but there must have been a great mental toll on them, living "*as close as the fingers on my hand*" for so long. Discipline was kept by the Acting NCOs, most of whom had little experience of controlling subordinates, particularly when those subordinates knew it. In some ships the soldiers were grouped together in sixes to look after their own tiny areas. John Luard on the *Marchioness of Ely* in 1822 reported that they were paraded and inspected each day to make sure they and their berths were clean. Some days the men paraded without boots or stockings to make sure their feet had been washed. But washing facilities were meagre and sea water was used so nobody ever felt fresh. How Eliza washed her whole body cannot be imagined. On fine days they were allowed on deck in groups and some showered up there in full view of the whole company. This gave them precious time to stretch, walk about and admire the endless horizon.

Of course, all things are relative and, as we must constantly keep reminding ourselves, we must not judge the past by today's standards. The ship's crew no doubt had accommodation even more cramped. As many were on duty at any one time they probably just hopped into any vacant and warm bed at the end of a day. But their days were busy, active and outdoors, not with long hours of boredom and enforced idleness. When on shore they lived in doss-houses, just as cramped, and thought it normal, or with their families in one room and no sanitation. Our soldiers probably came from similar backgrounds. Our Family was used to communal living but for them it was the enforced imprisonment, the constant press of sweaty bodies and the constant fear of living with just one plank between them and eternity. And this was very much a man's world, especially on board a ship, and most men considered that women entered it at their own peril.

It was two days before *Macqueen* weighed anchor and moved out towards the main channel of the River Thames and anchored. It was another four days before the log recorded that they came out of the river and anchored again. The main delay was caused by being becalmed in fog for two days. It wasn't until 24th January that *Macqueen* "*left England*" and fell abreast Dungeness. On 31st she anchored off Cowes on the Isle of Wight. No reason is given except the taking on of 444 gallons of fresh water.

After these early days of too little wind or only light breeze, the weather changed dramatically off Cornwall. On Tuesday 3rd February, Our Family's twentieth day on board, the log reported a fresh gale, hard squall, rain and high seas and that "*the ship is labouring much and shipping several large seas*". In other words, the huge waves were breaking right over the ship.

Down below, on the crowded bottom deck, the deafening noise, frightening bangs, creaks and crashes, the dramatic movement of the ship, the stench of fearful bodies and vomit, for hours on end must have been dreadful. No food could have been delivered but nobody could have kept it down. Everything had to be battened down tight but still water would have poured through small gaps and around the hatches so everything was soaked. Their quarters were probably under at least a foot of water. And in early February it would have been so cold. The small swinging oil lights would have been extinguished for fear of fire and it would have been pitch black. All the livestock, normally penned on deck, would have been brought down for fear of being washed away so the squealing of the pigs and horses would have added to the pandemonium.

Every Sunday divine service was held unless it was too rough but even though this was a Tuesday the log reports that there was "*too much wind and sea to perform divine service*". Every passenger must have been calling for God's help as they wondered what sort of hell-hole they were going to die in.

The weather eased as they tacked past the Lizard lighthouse at the tip of Cornwall and out into the open ocean. Two days later it had picked up again to a fresh gale, high seas and heavy swell and in the afternoon a seaman fell overboard about 160 miles WSW of Land's End. The ship hove to and a boat was lowered and picked him up. He was extremely lucky. Those below knew little of such events. One of their many unpleasantnesses must have been the lack of knowledge of what was going on, not even a view of the outside watery world. They could only put their faith in God, the Commander and his crew.

After all this drama, life on board *Macqueen* settled into a routine. The worst was over. On 17th February Madeira was sighted from the crow's nest and on 21st it was Tenerife. The ship's log recorded the vital routine of constant trimming and adjusting of sails which were the engine and steering of the ship. This went on day and night. The sailmaker and carpenter were often aloft doing repairs. Every Sunday the ship was pumped out and the remaining drinking water was recorded, bearing in mind that the barrels were filled if it rained.

Washing the decks, particularly the gun deck was carried out every Sunday and often sometimes twice in between. Keeping the whole ship in good order, down to small details, was important. Keeping the crew and soldiers in good order was maintained by physical punishment for theft, insolence or disobeying orders. Each miscreant was confined and allowed out within a day for a Court of Enquiry. The standard punishments were two or four dozen lashes with a cat-o-nine-tails although the Marine Boys were let off with a whipping. Two army recruits got away with two dozen lashes for riotous behaviour. In all eight men were punished but only one man, an army recruit, was disciplined twice and he was rewarded with 6 dozen lashes the second time.

Sightings of "*strange ships*" were always recorded and, if close enough, a boat was put down to visit. The whole ship's company was mustered every Sunday. They were brought on to the deck by divisions and the taller men had a chance to stretch up and touch the vast sky and sea all around them.

On Thursday 11th March, day 56, the equator was crossed for the first time. The log records the weather was calm at noon and progress was slow but there is no mention of this as a special day. Their longitude puts the ship exactly in the middle of the Atlantic Ocean, mid-way between Africa and South America. The crew took her far out to sea get the best, steady trade winds, to avoid currents and avoid pirates who plied off the African coast. In 1823 there were only a few disease riddled slave ports on the west coast of Africa and nothing was known of the interior. It was to be more than 50 years before Stanley made his fantastic journey across the centre of the continent and it began to open up. Africa was irrelevant to Macqueen and her passengers and best avoided.

Did Our Family, down below, know they were crossing the equator? Did someone come down and tell them? Was there a ceremony? What were they doing to while away the time? Such things were not recorded on the ship's log. There was no space for any sort of activity or exercise for the recruits and it must have been stiflingly hot. The boredom must have been intense.

For six days as they approached the south of Africa they had *"Duchess of Atholl in company"*; this ship being a sister to *Macqueen*. The two ships were twins in every respect and on the same journey. *Duchess of Atholl* was carrying infantry. Then the journey took *Macqueen* over 250 miles south of The Cape, following west to east along latitude 39 for sixteen days before turning north up the middle of the Indian Ocean.

On the night of Saturday 7th May, day 113, *Macqueen* crossed the equator for the second time. There was a pleasant breeze and she was sailing well. But this was a momentous crossing because, as the ship's log records;

> *"At 9am. Eliza, wife of Thomas Little (recruit) was delivered of a son"*

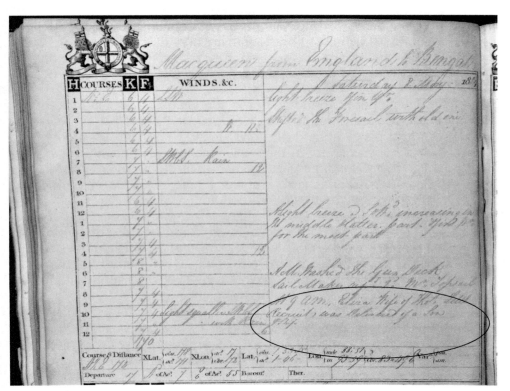

Macqueen's log of 7th May 1824. A light breeze for the most part, washed the gun deck, Sail Maker repaired the 2nd Main Topsail, a boy was born.

Among the dreadful heat and cramped conditions, the sea-sickness and the morning-sickness, the fear of the voyage and the fear of a first birth, with 200 unwashed and uncouth men looking on, a baby boy was born. He was, in fact, the third child to be born on board, each a boy and each recorded with the same brief report, which didn't give their names. So the recruits now had three crying, mewling and puking babies to disturb them. In our antiseptic, prim and proper 21st century world it would be nice to think the surgeon allowed Eliza to climb the ladders up to his apartment to have some peace and dignity in her labours but there is no indication of this and it is likely that he let nature take its course helped by the other women below.

As if to recognise the new birth, that afternoon saw the onset of an early monsoon, blowing strongly from behind. On the following day it carried *Macqueen* the furthest distance in any one day of the voyage; from latitude 1.46 to latitude 6.39, a distance of about 300 miles. There was thunder and lightning and divine service was cancelled because there was too much wind and the weather was unsettled.

The following Sunday, 15th May, depth soundings were being taken hourly and *Macqueen* met up with the *Duchess of Atholl* again. On Monday a pilot came aboard and on Tuesday 17th May *Macqueen* moored at a buoy offshore in the 'New Anchorage' Hooghly River, the main port of Calcutta. The journey was safely over and the writers and cadets went ashore. But it was not yet over for the army recruits who remained on board for another twelve days.

Macqueen left England with 375 souls on board and it is recorded on arrival that 378 went ashore so we know that all the little boys at least survived to venture into their new land. Deaths were frequent on voyages, through illness or accident, and the fact that nobody died on this voyage could be counted as a success.

During these twelve days work increased for the crew as the ship had to be scrubbed, caulked, pumped out and made to look perfect. Also the cargo was slowly unloaded onto sloops and taken ashore. This was done by native labour and *Macqueen's* crew had shore leave. Two of them were brought back to the ship by Calcutta police. Unfortunately, that was not all that was brought back. In the weeks that followed as *Macqueen* was unloaded and loaded again disease was brought on board. From 9th to 22nd July, seven of the ship's company died, including a Quartermaster and the surgeon's servant. No cause is given, probably because it was not known, but they picked up something in the town, from the food or local water or just by mixing with the natives.   Others were sent ashore for treatment, so the outbreak was widespread. All this was to be expected. It was accepted that several new arrivals in every contingent of army recruits would die within the first few weeks, succumbing to new disease to which they had no resistance.

It was at 1pm on Saturday 29th May that Our Family and all the other recruits stepped out into their new and dangerous world. But while they sat in their 'prison', at anchor for twelve days it gives us time to look at the background to life in India and here we must condense nearly a millennium into a couple of pages.

These 4 illustrations by James Baillie Fraser were drawn in about 1824-5 and show Calcutta, the city to which Our Family was heading. New buildings were springing up as British rule approached its peak. The views seem designed more to impress than reflect the human reality of what would greet our arrivals, just as the picture of Dromoland on page 23 does not represent the lives of the mass of the population.
1. The Town Hall.   2. Loll Bazaar and the Portuguese Catholic Chapel.
3. Government House.   4. The Writers' Building – government offices.

INDIA

CHAPTER 5

BRITISH INDIA

Thomas and Eliza and their companions were to find a very different world on their arrival in Bengal but they would see many similarities too. As we see the injustices of Ireland, by today's standards, there were enormous injustices in India too but, even more than in Ireland, they were generally accepted by the indigenous people at that time.

India was ruled by a British private company, The Honourable East India Company (The Company), not by the British nation. It was The Company Army that Thomas and the others had joined. The Company had been formed by a royal charter in 1600 and was granted, by Elizabeth 1, the right to trade in the whole world to the east of Africa. Its remit therefore was to trade with all nations from the Cape of Good Hope as far as The Spice Islands and China. At the beginning this trade was dominated by the French and the Dutch and it was over a hundred years before The Company gained dominance and established its main trading ports in India by fighting and defeating the French and Dutch and negotiating its own trade deals with local rulers. It was in the hundred years before Thomas arrived, since about 1725, that The Company had grown to a position of ruling the vast area we know today as India, Pakistan, Bangladesh and, later, Burma. It was bordered to the west by, again using today's names, Iran and Afghanistan, to the north by China and Nepal and to the east by Thailand.

India had never been a unified nation such as we know today, just as Europe was a mass of small nation states. England had been conquered in 1066 by Normans and in the 1400s England ruled half of what is now France. Parts of Spain were ruled by the Moors, for 800 years until 1492. It wasn't until the formation of the Holy League in 1684 that the Turkish muslim threat to the whole of Europe was overcome, they having reached nearly to Vienna. Until the 1870s Germany and Italy consisted of dozens of autonomous states which often fought among themselves. Borders changed as allegiances changed and kingdoms were in a constant flux as powers of rulers waxed and waned. The battle of the Boyne in 1690 and its resulting treaty of 1697 set the scene for life in Ireland for 250 years until that state fought to release itself from foreign rule. As recently as 1939 a European state had thought it had the right to expand into other states and the resulting war lasted nearly six years and cost tens of millions of lives. There was Yugoslavia in the 1990s and even in 2022 the old human story continues on and on in Ukraine.

Early British adventurers found a similar, familiar situation in India. There were dozens of principalities governed by different races with their own languages, religions, currencies, customs and castes. There were Muslims, Hindus, Sikhs, Pathans. The Pathans from the north-west were, for example, further divided into Afridis, Mahsuds, Mohmands and Wazirs. From 1526 to 1707 the Mohgul Empire violently fought its way into India and then, just as violently was driven out. Their motive was pure aggressive military expansion. Rulers changed as their power waxed and waned over decades and centuries just as in Europe. The wars were bloody with no mercy shown to a defeated army which had to be annihilated in order for the new regime to gain power. Old rulers were deposed, often multiple times in a principality over the centuries, and their wealth was appropriated or carried off by the victors. The British, in the form of The Company, were just the latest in a long line of new rulers but they tended to inveigle their way in to power by trade negotiation at first, then coercion, then wars as a last resort. They muscled in over many decades, rather than conquer suddenly by brutal military force. As time went on the idea grew among the British that they had a divine right to bring the benefits of their unifying civilisation, rule of law, infrastructure and trade to less developed countries such as India.

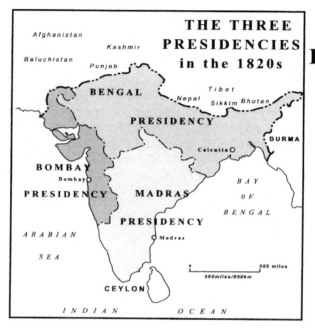

THE THREE
PRESIDENCIES
in the 1820s

**BRITISH
INDIA
in the
1820s**

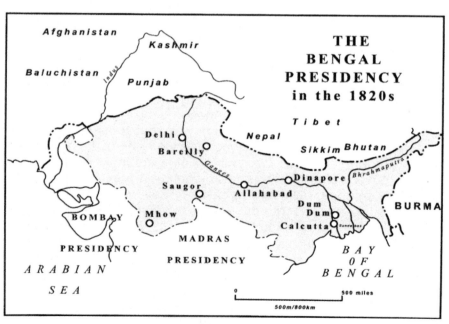

THE
BENGAL
PRESIDENCY
in the 1820s

The Company divided its territory into three Presidencies; Bengal, Madras and Bombay. Our Family went to the Bengal Presidency. At the time they joined, The Company was still expanding and consolidating its territory but the years that Our Family were there were, fortunately, quiet militarily in Bengal. The most recent major war had been the Third Maranatha War of 1816 – 1819 that had secured the western border. It was then relatively quiet for Bengal until the disastrous war in Afghanistan in 1837, the year that Thomas and Eliza left. This was the first ever major defeat of a British army. The First Burmese war of 1824 - 6 was particularly bloody on both sides but it was fought by troops from the Madras Presidency so did not involve Bengal armies.

Perhaps Our Family thought they were unfortunate not to be involved in a major war. The young bucks may have relished a good fight in which they could put all their artillery skills to proper use but they were best out of it as casualty rates were often 50%, even among Company soldiers.

India, including modern Pakistan and Bangladesh, with a population in 1820 of 210 million (1.76 billion in 2020), was ruled by a tiny European population of 41,000 of whom 37,000 were in the army. This incredible proportion in the army is explained later when we discuss the many non-military jobs that soldiers performed. These British members of the army were outnumbered 5 to 1 by native troops who voluntarily served The Company. Nearly 200,000 native Indians were employed in The Company army for much the same reasons as British men joined up. Another simple and basic reason for the loyalty of British Native troops was that they were paid on time. This is how the continent was overcome, bit by bit, by so few British. The armies of the individual local rulers that The Company had fought were often made up of mercenary troops divided within themselves by race, religion and caste. They were unreliable and disorganised, compared with the united, disciplined Company Army. The British strategy of "attack first and fast" intimidated the local troops who lacked decisive leadership. The Company remained and was accepted because it did not force change. It was primarily interested in trade and this was not helped by rocking the boat. It allowed most customs to continue, did not interfere with religions or the caste system and until about the 1840s got on quite well with the native population, as long as they knew who was boss.

Changes of rulers had little effect on ordinary people. They were poor and their lives were tough. They were taxed, treated well or badly and there was nothing they could do about it. They were more concerned about the weather, their crops and about being left to get on with their lives. Brigadier General Neville Chamberlain was up in the NW Frontier and talking to an old chief who told him,

> *"Many conquerors, like the storm, have swept over us and they have passed away leaving only a name and so it will be with you. While we poor people, like the grass, remain, we lift our heads again."*
> 1858, taken from his 1909 memoir and recounted in *'Sahib, The British Soldier in India'* by Richard Holmes, page 42

Europe and India were similar, both with their princely states, rulers and ruled, wars and peace, religious conflicts, famines and plenty. That's how the world was.

In the distance, to the north of our recruits on Macqueen, up the Hooghly River, was the magnificent and extraordinary city of Calcutta, one of the largest cities in the world – "The City of Palaces". Thomas and Eliza and their brothers would have been amazed by it so it is worth a quick description. Two facts stand out.

The first thing that would have struck Our Family when they first visited was the buildings. Since the beginning of the century swamps had been drained around Calcutta to enable it to erect grand new administrative buildings and parks which emphasised the power and permanence of British rule. But it was the grand houses of the wealthy that dominated and would have seemed to be palaces to the native population and probably to Our Family too. Some of these buildings are shown in the illustrations on pages 51, 52, 58 and 61. As in London these fantastic structures were built in open fields and only later were surrounded by new buildings as the city engulfed them. The Company left people to their own devices in terms of planning and style, as was the case in most British towns, but this resulted in haphazard development and few and unplanned services – even few paved roads in the city. Among the grand houses were small shanty towns of their servants. However, by the 1820s some sense of order was beginning to emerge.

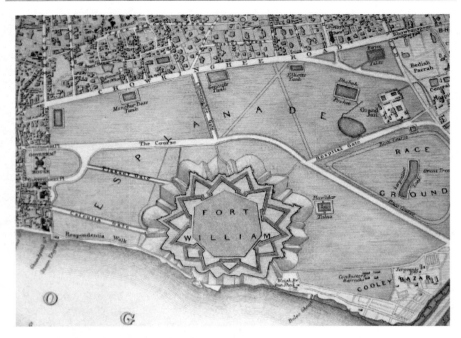

Above - An 1844 plan of Fort William and its Esplanade.
Below - An 1828 painting by William Wood showing some of the barrack buildings and St Peter's Church.   British Library

The city was dominated by the vast Fort William which Our Family would visit regularly in later years. This was the military centre, the military headquarters of all Bengal. It was completed in 1781 and was in the form of an irregular octagon with walls designed to reflect cannon shot. The fort itself covered an area of 1.9 square miles, (5sq km), approximately two miles (3km) in length and over half a mile (1km) wide. It was surrounded by a dry moat 30' (9m) deep and 49' (15m) wide and then by an open parade ground, called the Esplanade.

Secondly, as Our Family were to get to know Calcutta better they would have been amazed and perhaps confused by its Cosmopolitan population. The population of the City of Calcutta in 1837, in its first reliable census, was 229,705, and its suburbs held another 217,193. London, the largest city in the world, had a population of 1,878,000 in 1831 and Calcutta had overtaken the city of Dublin, with its population, in 1831, of 204,000. The census took eight months to complete and some of its detail was disputed at the time but the broad picture it paints was what Our Family would have got to know. The chart shows the diversity of Calcutta's inhabitants and throws a light on the

Population of Calcutta by Race 1837		
	City	Suburbs
English	3138	
Eurasians	4746	
Portuguese	3190	
French	160	
Europeans		740
Armenians	636	
Jews	307	
Moguls	509	
Parsees	40	
Arabs	351	
Mugs	683	
Chinese	362	
Madrassies	55	
Nat. Christians	49	
Hindoos	137651	138363
Mahomedans	58744	61054
Low Castes	19084	
Natives		15801
East Indians		1235
Total	229705	217193

"Population and Mortality in Calcutta", W H Sykes, Journal of the Statistical Society of London, March 1845

multitude of languages, accents, dress, customs, religions and lifestyles that Thomas and Eliza would never have experienced in Loughrea or even London, if they had managed a quick visit while there. This diversity brought about what was known as the Bengal Renaissance during which intellectuals of totally different backgrounds debated the great matters of the day. A growing number of Indians had become wealthy by providing for the extravagant lifestyles of Europeans and, in fact, most of the land in Calcutta was owned by Indians and leased to the Europeans. By 1831 there were twelve English language newspapers, from daily to weekly, with high circulations that can only have meant they were bought by many westernised Indians. On the other hand, The Asiatic Society existed to encourage knowledge of all things Asian as many Europeans were interested in Indian culture. Important leaders of Calcutta society, such as the British Prinsep family and the Indian Tagore family, with whom Thomas was to be associated in years to come, were prominent members. At a less intellectual level, the wealthy flaunted their affluence in grand balls, concerts and other entertainments. In the 1820s, professional musicians and actors raised the standard of local productions. A Mechanics Institute had been set up, followed in 1823 by a Medical and Physical Society, both aimed at encouraging Indians to become skilled in these areas. A Library Society was started in 1819, opening a public library in 1836, for which Europeans paid a subscription but Indians could use it free of charge. Many European ladies were involved in charitable works by the 1820s and schools, hospitals and orphanages were set up.

Of course, the other noticeable fact to be drawn from this is that the 3138 English (presumably meaning British) in the census, made up of 1953 men and boys and 1185 women and girls, ruled Bengal and were the dominating culture. If, from the 1953 males, one removes perhaps 250 soldiers in the barracks of Fort William and the boys (most of whom were sent to Britain for education), it can be seen that the ruling group of men did not number much more than about 1250. There were also officials in the provinces.

None of this would have been noticed by Thomas and Eliza in their early days but they were certainly involved with these people and their society later. They would also experience a downside of Calcutta society – its rigid respect for class and hierarchies.

This sketch, entitled 'The Town and Port of Calcutta' was drawn by Sir Charles D'Oyly in 1848. It shows the grand city in the background and, even 25 years after Our Family landed there, ships waiting to be unloaded by small boats. There are traditional fishermen and grand Europeans going past in their carriages on the unmade road.

INDIA

CHAPTER 6

MILITARY LIFE – ON THE MARCH

Now we must go back to our recruits, stuck on board for twelve whole days, and no doubt anxious to get going. They were allowed on deck in groups as long as they didn't disrupt the unloading of cargo, and the scene must have been fascinating compared with endless miles of flat horizon they had seen briefly while at sea. The port of Calcutta was enormous with ships arriving and leaving on most days. But everything was different. This was their first sight of the hundreds of semi-naked native workers unloading everything by hand and carrying it away. Their carts were pulled by oxen or buffaloes and Thomas and Eliza would have wondered at the working elephants and camels. They would have been assailed by men in bumboats selling them fruit, trinkets and all sorts of wares, shouting up to them in an English they struggled to understand.

The recruits would have had to grow accustomed to the heat on their voyage but this was the reality of their new land. April, May and June were the hottest months, with temperatures normally ranging from 27 °C to 36 °C but sometimes reaching above that. The end of May also saw the start of the monsoon season when even the wind was hot and the humidity would have been increasing making it very unpleasant. No wonder that a few from every consignment of newly arrived soldiers would die of the heat during these first months or of a disease to which they had no immunity.

Nevertheless, on Saturday 29th May 1824 they all donned their woollen uniforms with high tight collars for the 10 mile (16km) march to the Artillery Headquarters at Dum Dum. It was their first march after four months on a cramped ship so with lack of exercise and the strange sensation of being on firm ground, this must have been a great ordeal. What did they expect to see? Had they dreamed of Rajas in fine clothes, palaces and ornately decorated elephants? Most recruits report their great disappointment. One Sergeant Major considered it,

> "Hotter than Hades and a damned sight less interesting".
> (British in India, p.145)

Others just commented on the beggars, the dust and mud when it rained, the sweat that poured from them and the thousand flies that stuck to it.

Our group were soon out of the docks and, bypassing Calcutta, was soon marching through flat, open countryside that had been partly developed for agriculture since the barracks were built in the 1780s. Behind the marching column, walking less formally, were the wives. The landscape is described in *The Asiatic Journal and Monthly Miscellany* of March 1834 as unattractive and uninteresting but everything would have been new to our soldiers. They would have passed several large houses owned by wealthy natives, each with a verandah and surrounded by ornate gardens. One owned by a Raja had an extensive menagerie, the largest in Bengal. Four miles from Dum Dum was the magnificent and splendidly furnished mansion of Dwarakanath Tagore, a *"very rich and highly intelligent native gentleman who has embraced the European way of life and holds lavish parties for his European and Native friends"*.

Thomas would never have imagined, on that first day, how, in years to come, he would be involved in business with this great man, the head of one of the most influential Indian families.

But on they marched and along the way they would have been amazed by the local wildlife; the colourful birds and monkeys, the wandering sacred cows and the elephants, and the strange vegetation. As they approached the town of Dum Dum they would have seen the houses of senior officers and the spire of the recently built Anglican church and their first sight of the town showed that it consisted of low dwellings of the natives who served the barracks.

Finally, they marched in to barracks themselves. Accommodation for the troops consisted of single storey buildings, each with its verandah for shade and positioned next to the maidan, or large grass square used for artillery practice. On other sides of the maidan were houses of the officers and messes. Dum Dum was a cantonment or permanent building to house troops and equipment and these were being built at major centres up the Ganges to the north. They were all of similar grand style and built to impress the locals and demonstrate British permanence.

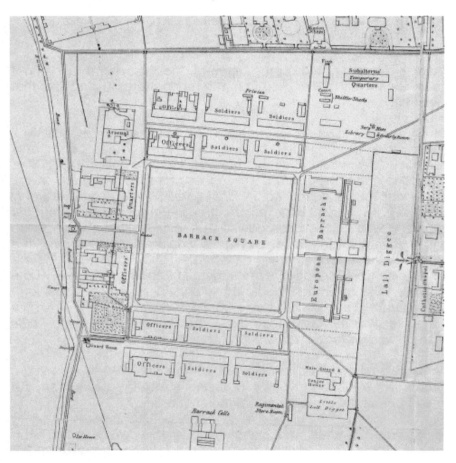

A plan of the Cantonment and Civil Station at Berhampoor in 1859 but that at Dum Dum would have had a similar layout. The parade ground was about 500 yards / 460 metres square. Architecture Beyond Europe Journal. Opposite is the same place in 1809, not long after it was built and perhaps before it was completed. But it gives an idea of the style of buildings.

In typically florid style *The Asiatic Journal's description* goes on:-

> *The mess room and its accompaniments form a very superb building, affording suites of apartments on a far more magnificent scale than those belonging to any European barrack. The splendour of Woolwich fades before the grandeur of Dum Dum.*

At last, it seems, Our Family had arrived at somewhere pleasant as a new home. There were recreation rooms and even an extensive library and a whole floor was taken up by a ballroom and theatre often visited by society from Calcutta and other towns round about. There were balls once a month at which crowds of single young men stood around with little hope of a dance with only thirty or forty young ladies. The theatre occasionally attracted troupes of famous actors, some even from England.

There is evidence that these facilities were open to all ranks. There was less of a divide between officers and ranks in the Company army than in any branch of the King's Army but *The Asiatic Journal* also mentions that "*Hindoo youths*" put on amateur shows so it is most likely that ordinary soldiers did so too to the entertainment of their fellows. They must have suffered to some extent due to the great shortage of ladies but, as we learn later that Eliza was quite happy to sing for the entertainment of others, perhaps she had a part to play. But ladies were not needed for field days and grand reviews which took place on the maidan in the cooler months and which also attracted spectators from elsewhere.

It was about this time that The Company first began to consider the comfort of troops and thought of tackling their boredom. An 1804 report by Dr Robert Jackson was the first to connect soldiers' health with their built environment and building specifications laid out details of ventilation, shade, etc. Walls were to be of a certain thickness and whitewashed, verandahs were to be 20 feet (6m) wide. Dum Dum being the largest such Barracks may have been the first to install such benefits and perhaps it was to publicise this that *The Asiatic Journal* wrote this report. Our Family arrived as these improvements were being introduced.

Our Family also arrived a year after the consecration of a Catholic church in Dum Dum, a great rarity which had been built by subscriptions from resident Catholics who recognised the need of so many of the Catholic soldiers based there. The significance of this was that Britain and The Company feared the effect of so many Irish Catholics in the Army as the Irish, in general, were considered not loyal to the Crown. Yet The Company was dependent on them. They also feared religious conflict which could be ignited among the many native religions by evangelical Christians. The influx of Irish Catholics placed them in the middle of The Company's dilemmas, particularly as they bonded together as a group and supported each other in any grievance, almost like a modern Trade Union. A major Irish grievance had been the lack of English and Gaelic speaking Catholic priests, although this had been as much a grievance with Rome as it was with The Company. This new church was a breakthrough, even before Catholic Emancipation in Britain in 1829, and the Army even paid the priest's stipend. Catholics, after all, had been in India since the 6th century, were a familiar part of Indian life and, although they welcomed converts, they were not active evangelists.

However, our men were there with a job to do and, being raw recruits, they had to learn their trade. Much of their instruction and practice was carried out in the early morning and late evening to avoid the midday heat. For the first year our four men were together in 2 Battalion, 7 Company, in Dum Dum so they would have started together with practice in firing a musket. This involved tipping gun powder into the priming pan, snapping the lid shut, loading the ball and pressing the trigger which would hopefully create enough spark to ignite the powder and fire the ball. At under 100 yards (90m) the aim could be accurate and there was a good chance of hitting one of a row of men, if the gun was held steady. There was practice on bayonet combat at close quarters – quick, straight thrusts.

But this was the Artillery so Thomas and the others had a lot more to learn. Their main guns at this time were 18 pounders and heavy howitzers and they had to achieve a rapid rate of fire which was exhausting as it involved loading each time while manoeuvring the guns to correct aim and range. There were different types of ball and shell; roundshot, canister and shrapnel, each with a different effect and range. At the time of Thomas' arrival some artillery was still being pulled by slow, lumbering oxen but horses were rapidly taking over due to their speed and manoeuvrability. This was another skill to be learnt as stopping speeding horses too quickly could mean them being over-run by the heavy gun they were pulling. Much of the heavy work was done by Native troops but British troops needed the skill to command their team.

Finally, they had to learn the instructions beaten out by the drums because drummer boys were not musicians, they were key communicators in the heat of battle.

Practice, practice, practice could soon become boring so what could occupy the men in their spare time and what could they spend their pay on? The obvious answer is drink and with so many lone men, there often developed a laddish drinking culture which seemed to be acceptable to their officers who were often no better. The drink of choice was arrack, a local fire-water, and men were issued with a daily ration. More was available in the canteen or bar or could be bought from those who chose not to drink their ration.

Team sports were increasingly popular in the public schools of Britain as a means of toughening up the elite British youth so they could safeguard the future of the Empire but there was little formal organisation and such activities had not developed among ordinary troops in the 1820s. Hunting and shooting were encouraged as a way of improving aim. Large tracts of land were unpopulated and teaming with game, from tigers to bears and deer but they often fought back and this was another easy route to an early death; one of many we shall hear about as our story proceeds. Another very popular sport was pig-sticking which developed formal rules along the lines of fox hunting. Keeping your eye on a boar while chasing it at speed on a horse was dangerous. One gulley or stump and the rider would be on the ground and, unique among chased animals, the boar often turned round and attacked, which added to the thrill and the danger. It was almost exclusively officers who took part in these sports and good horse was prized like a fast sports car is today. Ordinary soldiers had no horses but it is fair to assume that Thomas learnt to ride later and probably took part in such sports. At least Our Family could read and use the library but men who took up gentler activities such as collecting the large and colourful butterflies were often ridiculed as sissies by their rowdier mates.

These two drawings by Captain RSS Baden-Powell in 1889 show the thrills and dangers of pig-sticking. A wounded hog would be very dangerous for a man on the ground.   National Army Museum

A great benefit of life in India, almost unique to the Irish, was their community spirit. Men tended to create groups of friends based on their home town or area. They knew each other's villages and local traditions, where they had worked in Ireland and, often, their families. They looked after each other, sent messages home for them. Even without a church, they would pray together and they were more generous in acts of charity. Many of the sectarian divides of home were lost in India and this common bond extended between Catholic soldiers and Irish officers, most of whom were from Protestant land owning families. Irishness and supporting each other was more important than rank or old grievances, many of which were left behind in Ireland.

But we must return to the underlying problem of boredom, reduced by drinking, gambling and loose women. With food, clothing and accommodation provided, how were the men to use their pay? Native brothels were cheap but also dangerous and more than a quarter of soldiers suffered from syphilis. This number increased to over half in the 1850s when the army was prevented from carrying out medical checks on the ladies of the brothels by a puritanical campaign in Britain that said such checks showed an official approval of these houses of sin. But what were the men to do when they outnumbered British women by more than ten to one and it was so difficult to get permission to marry? All this led to the soldiers' reputation among Calcutta residents for drunkenness and violence. In the barracks men were constantly sparring with each other, sometimes violently, but quickly made it up in the bar afterwards. They had to keep up with the drinking. They invented games and tests of physical prowess and just mucked about. Many had a skill, such as fiddle or tin whistle playing, telling wildly improbable stories or singing. To many it was the only home they had ever known and their mates were family. Their pride in polishing their kit to perfection or finally getting their drill perfect was pride in this family.

Thomas was different because he had a wife who was probably a steadying influence. He couldn't be one of the lads. Unless he was as bad as the others and became a reformed man later, it is a reasonable guess that he was not in with all the blokes and their drinking. He had ambitions from an early stage. An immediate ambition may have been to get his and Eliza's accommodation out of the communal dormitory and this was easiest to do if he got some sort of promotion. Later we will learn that he had money so rather than frittering his pay away on immediate pleasures he may well have seen that, if he was going to get out of the barracks, he would need some savings behind him.

Eliza had duties of her own to perform to earn her keep. In the barracks she would have had cleaning or cooking duties and perhaps be expected to act as nurse to the many sick. In a life back in Ireland a woman was always busy, keeping house, helping with the crops or spinning but in Bengal the army provided everything and there was no task that she could perform that a Native woman wouldn't do much more cheaply – other than giving birth. So there was a great danger that women would become very bored, feel useless and often be very lonely. Living among so many ribald men who had very little respect for the women could be very demeaning. Some women fell into the foul ways of the men but others rose above this and earned a little money by doing jobs for some of the soldiers, such as mending, sewing or writing letters, and they put the money aside for a rainy day or better times. Some soldiers' wives grew flowers and developed a little garden to try to civilise their environment, perhaps following an example set by an officer's wife who had her own plot.

There were many who thought wives were a burden and distraction to a fighting force so the rules applying to them were as strict as those applying to the men. Women could be disciplined or struck off the roll of the married establishment. A husband was responsible for his wife's behaviour and he too could be disciplined if he was too weak to control his wife and children.

In the early months there was so much else to get used to in this new world. It was essential to get used to the local food which, although it may have been given English names, was nothing like the food from home. Our Family's diet back at home would have been largely potatoes and it seems they were fortunate enough to have this backed up by other vegetables and occasional meat. Potatoes were a rarity in India so they would have got used to rice. Milk, butter and cheese were from buffaloes so all tasted very different. British style bread was unachievable due to the poor quality of the wheat so chapattis were the substitute. They would have eaten more meat than in Ireland but what animal provided it? Buffalo or Brahmin cattle provided the beef but for soldiers these would have been beasts at the end of their working life and fed on the scrub grass rather than the green grass of home. The meat was very tough, a quality not improved by the inability to hang it to mature. In the heat, meat went putrid in a couple of days and refrigeration was many decades away. What was described as mutton, was in fact old goat. Pork was seldom to be had as it was unclean for Muslims and abhorrent to Hindus. If there had been an abundant shoot some deer or hare or strange birds may have made their way into the mess kitchen. Fruit and vegetables of many strange varieties were abundant. Maybe some, when they filled their bellies with another good plateful, wondered if those they had left behind at home had enough to eat.

But, as is being mentioned so often, all this is relative. The wives of the officers and gentry of the Company may have complained about the quality but our soldiers were not as fussy. The food was plentiful, which was more than most had known at home. The subtle distinctions of flavours were lost on them and nobody expected variety as long as the plate was full. After four months on a ship, anything tasted good.

There was also a need to learn how to relate to the locals and their strange ways. The natives who worked in the barracks or who were part of the army had learnt to adapt to the British but if Thomas ventured into the village or even into Calcutta he would have experienced India in the raw; the confusion, bartering, begging and the good chance of being cheated or even robbed. Junior officers had official lessons and a mentor to guide them in their first months but ordinary soldiers had to learn from their mates and by experience. Ordinary soldiers had less need or opportunity to go out alone. Thomas and Eliza may well have found disparity in incomes and levels of poverty not far different from those in Ireland. They may have compared the caste system, whereby a person's place in society, the job he could do or even with whom they could be seen, with the conflict between Catholics and Protestants at home. They would have been amazed at the variety of religions and their co-existence, usually on peaceful terms but with occasional violent flare-ups, and the many Hindu gods, their temples and shrines on street corners and even in the middle of the road. They would learn not to cause flare-ups themselves by appreciating that they could not stick a pig in a Muslim area. To give a cow a shove with a sword point or shoot a peacock would upset every Hindu. The policy of The Company was to interfere as little as possible in religious affairs although Thomas and Eliza were there when the practice of Sati, the burning alive of widows on the husband's funeral pyre, was banned in Bengal in 1829.

These three views, although drawn much later, are more true to life than those shown earlier and are closer to Thomas' and Eliza's experience. They are main roads down which they would have walked or marched through the throng. Even these drawings are sanitised and idealised, not showing the poverty, crowds, chaos and smells. Without any sanitation, these streets were much like those of Loughrea, but with intense heat.

Below: Clive Street by Sir Charles D'Oyly, 1848. This was the mercantile heart of Calcutta. It depicts a decaying Palladian mansion built in European style by an Indian trader muddled in with old thatched huts. British Library

On the right are two illustrations of Chitpore Road which led north to Dum Dum, Barrackpore and beyond. It was an Indian district with all the activity of shops and bazaar. British Library

Top Right: A very early hand coloured photograph by Frederick Fiebig, 1851. It shows a never-quite-finished grand house with Ionic columns among stalls of ordinary Indians. A woman sits on the pavement selling something.

Bottom Right: By William Simpson, 1867. This shows crowds of street traders, travellers, bullock carts, men carrying heavy loads and a crippled child, all typical of Indian life. He wrote, "In this bazaar hundreds of Englishmen have had their first conception of Eastern life realised face to face with the living facts".

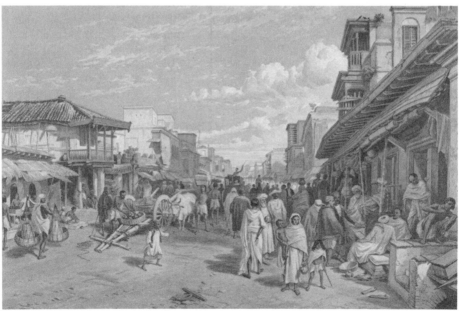

When they ventured forth Our Family would have come across the local currency which is another good example of the cultural differences they would have experienced. As explained in detail in the annual *Bengal Directory and General Register*, the local currency was the Rupee but in Bengal alone there were about a dozen different Rupees, loosely based on the locations of old Princely States. The official Company Rupee, that was used in all Company dealings throughout Bengal, was the Sicca Rupee, broken down as follows.

12 Pice	=	1 Anna
16 Annas	=	1 Rupee
16 Rupees	=	1 Gold Mohur

The official exchange rate was 1 Bengal Sicca Rupee equalling a British Half Crown, or 8 Sicca Rupees equalled one Pound sterling. In the towns around Bengal to which they were posted Our Family would have been confronted by different Rupees, all giving the locals an excuse to haggle and confuse. In the markets the currency among locals was the Cowrie Shell which fluctuated in value depending on how many were available at the time. Very roughly, about 5000 Cowrie Shells equalled one Rupee.

The Bengal Directory goes on to describe, over several pages, weights and measures, even more confusing than the currency. Weights and measures were different for different materials or liquids depending on what you were buying, where in Bengal you were or what type of shop you were in. Land measures varied by land use.

One of the great achievements of The Company was the unification of all these currencies and measurements across the whole of India but this was still a long way off in the 1820s. These details serve to illustrate the new and confusing environment that Thomas, Eliza and the others had to grow accustomed to in their first months in Dum Dum when they were all together in 2 Battalion, 7 Company. There were roughly 800 men in each Battalion which consisted of 10 Companies – or that was the standard practice but it varied widely. But it meant that the four brothers and cousins were close together in a unit of about 80 men, doing the same thing.

The Company Army produced an annual Muster Roll each June which shows what Battalion and Company each man was in. *The Bengal Register* lists where each Company was based so by matching the two it can be seen that by June 1825 William and Robert Little had gone together to Saugor and Michael Lally went to Bareilly where they stayed for at least two years. Both these postings were a long way from Dum Dum. Thomas had, by June 1825, been promoted and stayed in the Calcutta area and we shall return to him later. For now we will look at the movements of William, Robert and Michael.

Boating on the lake at Saugor. A tranquil scene.

Saugor was about 700 miles (1100km) west of Calcutta and Bareilly was about 800 miles (1300km) north west of Calcutta, near the western end of Nepal. The two towns were about 400 miles apart so Our Family was well and truly split up. Both towns were in sparsely populated fertile plains and both, particularly Bareilly, offered some respite from the heat in the winter. Calcutta's temperature was fairly even throughout the year as it was affected by the sea but, so far inland, Bareilly had much cooler winters, averaging between 10℃ and 20℃ in December and January – beautifully cool. To the north of Bareilly was the Terrai, a higher and cooler area of dense forest inhabited by bears, tigers and the great one-horned rhinoceros, second only to the elephant in size. If Michael was lucky he may have been posted on to the north, to Ranikhet which was a hill station and hospital in the utter beauty of the foothills of the Himalayas. For William and Robert, there were two great attractions in Saugor. The first was the magnificent fort, the vast round towers of which dominated the town and countryside for miles around. It was on the banks of a large lake that was itself surrounded by glorious Hindu temples and bathing places. They could have relaxed here, taken a boat out and enjoyed some peace.

But, you must be asking, how did they get there? The answer is that they marched. At about 12 miles a day, it took over two months. Time scales in those days were so very different to our experience today.

For Michael, the route from Dum Dum to Bareilly followed the Ganges, along what was euphemistically called The Grand Trunk Road, a 1,500 mile (2,400km) route into Afghanistan which had been travelled for 2,500 years. Its great advantage was that it was navigable all the way by carts and wagons but it was a wide, sprawling route of varying quality, diverting round obstacles and maintained only when it got bad enough to impede progress.

Soldiers on the march. They are awaiting removal of their camp as it is loaded on to camels. Those in blue are Artillery and those in red are Infantry. . . . . .

The Ganges itself was partly navigable but seldom used and totally impractical for large numbers of troops. It was simpler to march than load and unload boats. The large boats in use at this time were budgerows which were used to carry passengers or light and bulky freight such as cotton. They were flat bottomed, up to sixty feet (18m) long and powered by a square sail and by between twelve and twenty oars. Because of the vagaries of the river the crew would be frequently swimming or wading alongside to help steer it or towing it with ropes from the bank. The journey upstream from Calcutta to Allahabad took about three months. Downstream was much quicker but could be very dangerous. A budgerow must have been just one of the many extraordinary sights that Our Family saw in their travels and another example of how different life and culture were in India compared with Ireland. See the sketch of a budgerow on page 78.

William and Robert set off, on foot, across the great plains to the west. Most soldiers spent half of their lives on the march so it is worth describing these remarkable migrations which all Our Family would have undertaken. For every one soldier, British or Native, there were about five servants, or hangers-on, serving the Company as a whole. So if a Company of about 80 men was on the move, the whole caravan could consist of 500 people. A whole Battalion moving could mean 5,000 men and their animals taking a couple of days to pass any particular spot. Negotiating a narrow ford or rickety bridge could mean half the party camped nearby for days waiting their turn to cross. There were elephants to carry heavy loads such as guns and ammunition, whole trains of camels carried food, tents and equipment with pots and pans clanging as they went along. Separate camels carried the household effects of Officers; furniture and trunks of clothing. No British soldier would go near a camel as they were considered smelly, dirty, noisy and cantankerous so there were the horses carrying the Officers. Two

..... The bhysties, or water carriers, are filling their water bags from the river in which men are praying and washing.

or three men were responsible for each animal. This great crowd of men and animals had to be fed and watered with more people to do that. Everything had to be loaded and unloaded every day.

One of the reasons for so many servants was that their caste meant they would only perform a certain job. Some were born to be water carriers and they also had the responsibility to find water and keep their water bags filled. There were tent erectors who left first each day to ensure the next camp was ready. There were cooks and pot washers, tent and boot repairers. There were those whose job it was to bring in local fresh fruit, meat and milk, accompanied by endless haggling, not only with the locals from whom it was bought, but with the army cooks who needed it for their men. There were guards to look after all the money, for how else would the men be paid when they arrived? Our Family would have learnt very quickly in India that there would always be hangers on who lived by selling goods to anybody passing by – and here were perhaps 2,500 customers. They would disappear into nearby villages or climb trees and come back with fresh fruit and other items to sell to the soldiers as they marched along. And there were hangers on of a low caste, there to serve the servants of a higher caste. Some had families with them. And on and on the numbers grew.

At the end of this great parade were the wives; wives of Officers in pony traps or palanquins carried by six or four natives, wives of soldiers on foot. In wet weather they and the children trudged through the mud churned up before them. In dry weather they were

A budgerow on the Ganges by John Luard, 1843.

Just some of the amazing sights
Our Family would have become
used to.

By John Luard. The two in
colour were published in his
"Views in India, St Helena and
Car Nicobar, 1832 – 1838",

Serpent catchers and charmers.

An Indian dignitary proceeding
on an elephant.

Bhysties at a well.

coated and choked with the dust of hundreds of men and animals. Eliza was not on these marches to Bareilly and Saugor and probably never did one of 800 miles but this was the inevitable way she travelled, even if only for a few days or weeks.

In the hot seasons, which were most of the year, camp was taken down before sunrise so most travel could be achieved before it got too hot. Sometimes marching was only done at night. The men would be woken by drums, tents would be struck and rushed on ahead. Food would be ready to be served and drums would sound to fall in, and again to march. It was usually half an hour between waking and marching so there was some organisation in the chaos. There is no mention of washing. Water was too scarce and opportunities would be grabbed if a stop was called by a river when men would strip off and go in, even though most rivers in the north were freezing cold.

Gunner Bancroft made this same journey from Dum Dum in 1842, with 400 artillery recruits, so with a total party of perhaps 2,500. He reported the boredom of the march, often across uninteresting terrain, being alleviated by singing, jokes and practical tricks, at all of which the Irish excelled. Half the party was Irish and they had a gift of looking on the bright side. If things got out of hand, a couple of soldiers would break ranks to fight it out and, once it was proved who was right, they would just rejoin the squad and march on.

An officer in a palanquin. It takes ten men to carry and guard him.

Marching was hard. There was no leeway for weaker members. The Irish would have walked 25 miles at home without a thought but in India they sweated in tight breeches, woollen tunics, high stiff collars and tall hats. The ladies suffered from numerous tight fitting under garments and, although soldiers wives may have spared themselves this dignity, their long flowing dresses, whether dry or waterlogged would cling to their legs unless they hoisted them up and tucked them in. It often took only five minutes after reaching camp for a soldier to be asleep in his tent.

Death was an accepted part of the march, as it was at all times. Men just collapsed on the road from the heat or were so weakened by the march that they picked up strange diseases that finished them off. Where did the water carrier get his water from? The importance of water quality was not appreciated and a man could be up and marching in the morning and dead before he reached camp. Natives were called over to bury him and a detachment of his friends may go with them to find a place the jackals wouldn't dig up in half an hour. A quick "Hail Mary" and they marched on.

Crossing the Touse 1820   This is in the far north of India and away from main roads and paths. Troops could wait all day to go across one at a time. Perhaps an extreme example. From J B Fraser's Views of the Himala Mountains   British Library

Bareilly and Saugor were centres of the Company rule so it likely that William, Robert and Michael were sent to other towns or outposts in the regions. Later copies of *The Bengal Directory* are less clear about their precise whereabouts, often placing "*a Detail of Artillery*" in small places without saying what Company they were from. Detachments would be sent out to sort local disputes between tribes. Perhaps one tribe was stealing the crops or animals of another and this had to be stopped before it developed into a long running feud involving more and more tribes or villages. This was the soldiers' opportunity for a bit of action which they relished but more often than not the offending tribe would capitulate at first sight of the soldiers who would return disappointed. But William and Robert were close to each other, geographically, all their time in India, probably in Saugor for at least three years, then near each other in Fort William and Dum Dum later.

Michael Lally moved about more. He was a soldier for longer. In 1827 he was in Dinapore which was still in the north of the country. In 1828 he had moved 400 miles to Saugor. By 1830 he was most likely back in Dum Dum. In 1832 or 1833 he was involved in fighting near Barrackpore. This is known because, when he died in September 1833 his estate was paid the prize money allotted to soldiers after a successful military operation. This amounted to the princely sum of 3 Annas, 9½ Pice, a tiny amount so it was not a big battle and not much loot was carried off.

But we need to go back to Thomas and his promotion and the interesting fact that all Our Family members were promoted.

An ordinary soldier in the Company Army could only rise to a certain level, to Sergeant at the most. There was no way a Gunner, as the lowest rank was called in the Artillery, who showed particular talent could become an Officer. Officers bought their position even if it was the starting rank of Ensign. Haileybury School, in Hertfordshire, England, was founded in 1806 to train boys to become Officers and Senior Civil Servants in India and no common man could join their ranks at any stage. So what was an ambitious soldier, like Thomas, to do?

These two sketches are of villages on the road north of Calcutta along which William, Robert and Michael marched.
Top is of the village of Sheebpore by Sir Charles D'Oyly, published in 1848 in his 'Views of Calcutta and Environs'. In the middle is a small shrine.
Bottom is the village of Serampore by William Prinsep, 1848

INDIA

CHAPTER 7

FAMILY LIFE – AND DEATH

How did an ordinary soldier, like Thomas, better himself? All Our Family members managed to do this and they managed it because The Company Army did a lot more than fighting. This chapter looks at the personal lives of Thomas and Eliza and their brothers

The civil administration looked to the army for talented men to fulfil an enormous range of vital middle management jobs that the men who bought their way in from England were unsuited to or felt were beneath their dignity. The police and firemen were all soldiers and the middle management roles in the civil service and all sorts of public works were filled by soldiers. This filled a gap in the national administration but created a gap in the Army which Army Officers resented. They felt that their best men were stolen. However, this provided a unique opportunity for the common man to be promoted on talent alone. And there was no objection to Catholics. Nearly half of the Gunners were Catholics who would never get such an opportunity at home in Ireland where Catholics were prevented by law from such promotion.

Thomas was promoted within his first year in Bengal and this was very unusual. It was usually three to six years before a man proved himself worthy of being stolen by the authorities. This must demonstrate a particular ability, confidence and assertiveness on Thomas' part. By the annual Muster Roll of 30th June 1825 he was on 'The Town Major's List' in the Barrack Department in Fort William. By the following June he was a Sergeant in the Barrack Department.

This opens up one of the mysteries of India. What were the Town Major's List and the Barrack Department and what did men do in them? They are frequently mentioned but no record remains of their function. The Town Major's List showed everybody doing any job that was not directly military. The Barrack Department was one of the groups of such men and it is reasonable to assume that Thomas was doing an administrative job related to the Barracks. Whatever it was, it got Thomas out of the communal barracks and more importantly, it got Eliza out too. They would have had their own quarters, no matter how small, and the privacy to lead a proper married, family life. There was higher pay too and, in the relaxed atmosphere in The Company, opportunities to take on private jobs, on the side, if the day's work was not too arduous. Some men made a great deal of money in this way, either legitimately or by payments from interested parties in a particular project.

By June 1828 Thomas had joined the Public Works Department, 16th Division. It is more obvious what the Public Works Department did but, unfortunately, no records survive naming the tasks of individual members. Thomas is still recorded annually on the Army Muster Rolls but he was no longer a soldier.

There was much development work going on at this time. Ports were being expanded, roads and bridges built and drainage and irrigation schemes created. Military barracks were being rebuilt all over Bengal. In 1828 this effort was stepped up by the new Governor of Bengal, Lord William Bentinck. He was a great reformer. He made sati, female infanticide and human sacrifices illegal and made English the only language of the courts (rather than Persian) and of education (rather than dozens of local dialects). He founded the Calcutta Medical College, the first on western lines in Asia, and insisted it be open to everybody, regardless of race.

Under his rule, in 1833, the biggest project of them all was started; the metalling of The Great Trunk Road along its full length, at the enormous cost of £1,000 per mile. Communication in India was extremely primitive and this project was met with resistance from some English Governors and officials. They perhaps resisted for the same reasons that some landowners objected to railways in

Britain; that travel by peasants would open their eyes to opportunities and make them dissatisfied with their lot. In surveying opinions, it is said that one Bengal Collector complained that roads were unnecessary in his district because the people there did not use carts but carried everything on their backs or in panniers on the backs of bullocks. Even government despatches were carried on men's backs, hundreds of miles at 3 or 4 miles an hour. It was considered cheap and effective.

This paints another corner of the picture of life and attitudes surrounding Thomas and Eliza, but was Thomas involved in such works? It may have been that Thomas' role involved the care or breeding of horses as it was for this purpose that he was chosen to go to Australia and surely he would not have been chosen if he didn't have this skill. He was involved in horse racing in Australia so this must have been an enthusiasm engendered in India.

The job undoubtedly led Thomas to a predominantly outdoor life, the sort he would have been familiar with in Ireland, and this would have greatly broadened his mind. The soldiers' barrack room or the Officers' mess was a closed, male society. Its benefit was said to be that it developed the camaraderie of the troops and, by the re-telling of stories of their Battalion's days of glory, inculcated a deep loyalty to the Battalion. On the other hand, a crowd of men cooped up together in a closed environment with not much to do bred loutish behaviour, group-think and a mind closed to outside ideas and influences. Thomas, and the others, broke free from this and could expand their lives and minds in the varied and beautiful world around them. There were Public Works projects all over Bengal.

It was in 16th Division of Public Works, from 1828, that Thomas worked with Mathias Glynn who he had probably first met in Dublin when enlisting. They sailed together to India on *Macqueen* and were together in 2 Battalion, 7 Company in the first months in Dum Dum so knew each other well. Together they moved to 3rd Division Public Works in 1829 and worked together for four years, becoming good friends. Mathias was the same age as Thomas, 28 at this time, and came from Kilmacdough, about 18 miles (30km) from Thomas' home in Galway. Mathias' wedding records tell us he was in Mhow in 1828 so Thomas and Eliza would have been there too. Because of the tragedy that overcame Mathias, which we will learn about later, it is known that Thomas was in Dinapore in April 1831. In about the same year we know that Thomas and Eliza were in The

Sundarbans, east of Calcutta, because that is where their son, Thomas Jnr, was born. The rest of their travels are not known but this is indicative of a lot of travelling. Mhow is 1,000 miles (1,600km) west of Calcutta. Dinapore and The Sundarbans are 450 miles (725km) apart. They would have experienced the Grand Trunk Road but in a smaller group than previously described and maybe in a little more comfort. To get to Mhow would have taken nearly three months. The Sundarbans are out in the wild country and travel there would have been a lot more arduous.

Mhow was created as a town after the battle of Mahidpur in 1817 when the Holkars were defeated and the Princely State of Indore was taken by the Company. Mhow is situated on a high plateau and experiences very high temperatures in the summer, above 40 °C, and as low as freezing in the winter, which may have been appreciated by our soldiers. It was a remote outpost.

Dinapore is on the banks of the Ganges and lies in a vast, flat alluvial plain. Despite being about 375 miles (600km) inland the plain is only about 250 feet (75 metres) above sea level and was subject to frequent devastating floods. The Ganges is nearly four miles (6km) wide at this point and several large rivers flow down from Nepal and the Himalayas onto the plain and after floods they

Native Huts, from The Book of India, published in 1876

would often flow in new channels, altering the landscape. The land was fertile but the population was always on the move to new ground.

The Sundarbans is a vast remote area in the deltas of the Ganges, Brahmaputra and Meghna Rivers and also subject to frequent flooding. Its average height above sea level is only about 25 feet (7½m) and with a tidal range of up to 15 feet (5m) the whole area was subject to inundation. Was flooding a similarity that connected these two areas and may be a clue to Thomas work – in drainage and irrigation? This is probably a guess too far.

It is Thomas Jnr who said in later life that he was born in The Sundarbans which was a vast area of mangrove swamp, covering 6,500 square miles (17,000 sq km). It was largely uninhabited by humans but the home to a vast array of wild animals, notably the Bengal tiger, known for being a man eater, the large salt water crocodile which wasn't much better, and the Javan Rhinoceros. In Thomas' time unsuccessful attempts were being made to manage the forests and by the early 1830s over 100,000 acres (40,000 hectares) of uneconomic forest had been cleared for useful agriculture. It was not until 1875 that attempts to tame the area

A village in a clearing in the Sundarbans, drawn by Frederic Peter Layard after an original sketch of 1839

were abandoned and it was declared one of the first Reserve Forests. Even as late as 1911 it was not included in the census as it was considered a tract of waste country that had never been surveyed. So what was Thomas doing there? There were some towns on the northern fringes which were more easily accessible and perhaps they lived there, as venturing into The Sundarbans proper was for intrepid adventurers only. The journey there from Calcutta would have been along little used tracks and, once there, travel was almost exclusively by boat. What a place to take your wife when she is expecting, assuming they knew when they set out.

Thomas is recorded as holding this position in the 16th Division Public Works for another four years, making a total of about nine years in Public Works. He would have probably travelled extensively and seen much of Bengal. If he didn't enjoy the work he could have tried to change it. But he didn't and it would have been a wonderful existence and given him great satisfaction.

A traveller's bungalow, from The Book of India, published in 1876

His life would have been largely outside, just as he was used to at home. But where was home now? It is likely that Thomas' father died in 1830 and although the mail may have taken six months or more, we know they were in touch and would have had news from Ireland. The physical ties with Ireland were broken. Thomas and Eliza had come to a new home with their brothers and established themselves well now. Outside the monsoon season, as a junior civil servant, Thomas' office would have been his tent and his desk a collapsible table in the shade. He may have had clerks sitting on the ground with paper and ink horns and messengers ready to run off with letters. A native messenger with nothing to carry except letters could trot up to fifty miles a day if he was motivated. Thomas' superiors would have had a Company bungalow with furniture, carpets and decorations, and bathroom with servants to fill a zinc tub with cold water at the end of a hot day. Even many tents were fitted out in the same way. Then, as evening drew in, there would be drinks on the verandah but without ice. Ice was beyond man's ability out there. Many men like Thomas recorded that life could not be better than in the middle of nature's wonders, among the graceful forests or grasslands stretching as far as the eye could see. And an official bungalow or tent was always sited in a good spot, in the cool and with the constant sounds of hundreds of creatures all around. And there would, of course, have been a servant whose life was dedicated to ridding this idyllic scene of vermin, snakes and unpleasant insects.

This is all a pleasant but imaginary scene as we do not know exactly what job Thomas had or the level of superiority he reached. He was an ambitious man and it is known that in later years he was mixing with the great and influential men of Bengal society. Surely, he can only have met these people if he had risen to a high rank in the Public Works Department or had a successful business on the side, as was common. Thomas' and Eliza's life was now very different to life in the barracks.

It must also be said that it was not always as easy as this. There were very primitive tribes in some parts who objected to roads they didn't need or who objected to the benefits, such as irrigation, given to a neighbouring tribe but not to them. Their reaction was to fight over it and men like Thomas sometimes found themselves carrying out their non-military tasks in the centre of such hostility. As a last resort, the army would be called in to settle the dispute. One must also consider that it may have only been people who thought this life idyllic who wrote diaries and journals.

It is not possible to describe the lives of Thomas and Eliza with facts and suppositions alone and an attempt must be made to look at the way they thought nearly 200 years ago. Despite the obvious motivation of The Company to make a profit, there was a strong sense of duty in Victorian society. The British felt they had a divine mission to spread their knowledge, industry and civilisation to all parts of the world for the benefit of mankind and this often manifested itself most strongly among individuals, like Thomas, working with the locals. To build roads and bridges would benefit local people as well as The Company and their British constructors were often motivated simply by 'doing good'.

An example of this was Arthur Cotton who, as a young engineer, saw the terrible effects of a famine caused by drought in 1833 east of the Western Ghats. This experience motivated him to spend the next forty years building canals, aqueducts and dams. He was driven by a clear humanitarian vision, seeing this as the moral duty of rulers to care for their subjects. His irrigation systems still operate across fertile plains today, nearly 200 years later.

Spending years working closely with local communities, and vastly outnumbered by them, could build an affection for them and a rapport. It is likely that Thomas and Eliza learnt and appreciated the ways and needs of the local people and after so many years it is inevitable that they learnt the local language, probably more than one. This was often criticised as 'going native' but they had grown up with the desperately poor in Ireland. Most native servants were happy and eager to serve and Thomas and Eliza would have appreciated and respected this because they weren't born with the aloofness of many officers. In their later years they were great philanthropists, making great sacrifices for those less well off than themselves, so it is possible that this attitude developed in Bengal.

This is as much as is recorded about Thomas and Eliza in the ten years 1826 to 1835 but we shall return to their last two years in India later. All their brothers were promoted too and we can look now at brief records of each of their roles.

William Little was promoted in 1827. In fact, we know the exact date; 21st March 1827 which was less than three years after he arrived in Bengal. Like Thomas, he became a Barrack Sergeant in Fort William and in 1828 he is recorded as an Overseer Supervisor. He died in July 1830 in Fort William and his position at that time was given as Congr House Sergeant. It is not known what the abbreviation 'Congr' refers to or what these roles involved.

Robert Little was the next to be promoted. Until the Muster Roll of June 1829 he was a Gunner but in June 1830 he is listed as a Corporal in the Town Major's Department in Fort William, rising the following year to a Sergeant. By June 1833 Robert was a Sergeant in the Calcutta Town Guard, in other words he was a Police Sergeant. He held this position until he died in October 1835.

Michael Lally remained in the army. He was a Gunner until 1828. By June 1829 he had received a minor promotion and in 1832 or 1833 he was made up to Sergeant. This was a military Sergeant, the highest rank an ordinary soldier could attain, controlling Gunners, so he lived the military life all the time until his death in September 1833.

All these deaths! Only Thomas and Eliza lived to see their 30th birthdays. Did everybody die young in India? Attitudes to death were very different in the 1830s to attitudes today so it is worth looking at this. The fear of and expectation of death was such a common part of life to an extent that is difficult for us to comprehend today. They were brought up with frequent famines in Ireland and now their nearest and dearest were struck by strange illnesses and pestilence in India. it was all around Thomas and Eliza and one of the mysteries of their story is why they both survived when most people did not. This will move us on to the personal lives of each member of Our Family; their marriages and children.

There seemed to be a fatalistic indifference to death and an acceptance of the fragility of life and death's inevitability. Why should this not be the case when so little could be done to help a wounded or sick person. But this acceptance that little could be done seems to have led to little actually being done. The death rate in battle was frequently 50% and most died from wounds, even minor ones. If there was a field hospital, few ever came out alive as disease spread from bed to bed. Very few soldiers survived an amputation. The discovery of ether in 1846 and chloroform in 1847 showed that people were beginning to look for ways to mitigate the agonies people went through but it wasn't until the work of Pasteur and Lister in the 1860s that the value of extreme cleanliness became known. But all this was long after the time that Our Family was in India and did nothing to help them. The stench of gangrene and the cries of agony were often described as dreadful but never scandalous.

The records indicate that William and Robert Little and Michael Lally died of disease, rather than in battle but there was just as little defence against this than dying of wounds. So many diseases were unique or uniquely potent in India. Cholera could wipe out half a Battalion in a few days and with typhoid and malaria it made up the most common killers. Add to these beriberi, black water fever, bouton de Baghdad and other diseases for which the British had no resistance. Tetanus was caught from a simple infected cut. There were no cures for skin lesions, boils and ulcers brought on by the bites of sandflies and these could be debilitating and bring on death from other causes. In this frightening list were the killers of William, Robert and Michael, and their friend Mathias Glynn.

Without labouring this point, one must add the heat to the list of killers. Drills and parades were often held very early in the morning and marches often avoided the hottest part of the day, yet so many men died of heat stroke. It seems extraordinary now that alcohol was supplied in seemingly copious quantities to soldiers in the belief that it mitigated against heat stroke. Modern thinking must suggest that it made matters worse and the more you drank the greater stupor you were in as you cooked to death.

Such is the background to the lives of our Family and the statistics make you wonder why they ever chose to go to India. Before departure from Ireland they must have heard about the dangers of travel to and life in India. But if they had stayed in Ireland they may have died of hunger.

Sahib – The British Soldier in India gives a series of statistics in the chapter entitled 'A Familiar Friend'. A George Carter kept a record of deaths in the 2nd Bengal European regiment from 1840 to 1850. In these ten years the average strength of the Regiment was 732 men of whom 616 died – 84%. There was a total of 55 wives of whom 51 died, seven in childbirth – a worse percentage than the men. The Hon. Company's agents, Dodwell & Miles, published a list of the Company's Officers from 1760 to 1830 showing that only about 10% lived the 18 years to draw their pension.

This is backed up by your author's study of 207 deaths taken at random from around the records of the deaths of William and Robert Little, Michael Lally, Matthias Glyn and a James Lally who turned out not to be related. About 40 deaths from 1830 to 1835 were studied close to the record of each of these five. Only 8% of these deaths were of people over 40 years old. 14% were children under a year old and another 14% were aged 1 – 5. This 28% is much in line with the generally accepted figure of European infant mortality in India of between 30% and 40% before their sixth birthday.

Comparison with life expectancy in England demonstrates how much worse it was in India. In 1841, the first year for which such figures are available, a boy, at birth in England, would be expected to live, on average, until the age of 40 and a girl till 42. Their most dangerous time was in infancy. Deaths before their fifth birthday ran at 15%. If a boy achieved his fifth birthday he could expect to live to be 55 and a girl to 58. Deaths of under fives in India were more than double that in England. The latest figures for modern times are for 2011, when deaths in England under the age of 5 run at 0.4% and life expectancy at birth is 79 for boys and 82 for girls.

This discussion of deaths is worthwhile because it is so different to our modern existence where every death is to be avoided at all cost, because it is the termination of all existence, and every premature death is a scandal. In India in those days, when religious belief was such a fundamental part of thinking, most believed that death was part of life, a moving on to a new phase. Deaths were still a tragedy for parents, widows and orphans and the frequency of death affected every aspect of family life and the whole structure of society. And, of course, it was a reason for continuous recruitment in Britain. It was statistically likely that William, Robert and Michael would die within ten years of arrival. What was unlikely was that any one person should survive thirteen years, as Thomas and Eliza did. That they both, a married couple, survived for that long in India was unusual in the extreme. Was it luck or was there a reason?

Let's now look at the family lives of each member of Our Family and this will also bring in attitudes to marriage. The witnesses to the weddings indicate that Our Family stayed in touch, even if they travelled to different parts.

Thomas and Eliza are the easiest couple to study. They arrived as a married couple and lived together to move on from India after thirteen years. We know they had a child; a boy born, in May 1824, on the ship bringing them to India. The boy was recorded as coming ashore but no more is heard of him. He must have died. They had a son, Thomas Jr., in 1831 and another, William, in 1833 but we only know this because they survived to travel to Australia where records, such as of their marriage and death, gave their age. Typically, a married woman gave birth every eighteen months so there was time for two or three more children to be born to Eliza between 1824 and 1831, and maybe more after William when Eliza was still only in her mid-thirties. Catholic births, marriages and deaths were not required to be recorded in India until the late 1830s because they were outside the church of England. Even Anglican baptism records are not complete. Despite the Catholic Emancipation Act in Britain in 1829 and the number of Catholics in the army, Catholicism was not yet recognised in India in the 1830s. The needs of Catholics were mainly satisfied by Italian Jesuits or Portuguese priests. It must be assumed that Thomas and Eliza had the sorrow of losing at least three children in infancy. They would have had the additional sorrow of burying a child and having to move to a different posting, leaving the grave and knowing that nobody would tend it or care after they had gone.

William, Robert and Michael all married in India. It is important to look at the background to marriage in India before we look at the lives of these three because marriage was not undertaken in the same manner in India as it was in Britain and certainly not in the same manner as it is today.

A man's ability to marry was dominated by the dramatic shortage of women and this affected all levels of British society in India. British men outnumbered women by at least ten to one. The fact that all four of Our Family married was unusual but it is difficult to read anything into it. The great majority of men accepted a single life, though not necessarily celibacy.

Mixed marriages were common and generally accepted, as can be seen in the number of Eurasians in the 1837 census, and there were few places you could not take your Indian wife to, such as the Officers' mess. It was more difficult for an ordinary soldier to take an Indian wife because she would live in such close proximity to all the other men. India was divided much more by the Indian caste system and religions and by the British class system than by racism. Even the Bengal Club, founded in Calcutta in 1827 along the lines of a London club, had no barriers to race. It mattered little what race your wife was as long as she fitted in with your status. Many Officers took a bibi who was a partner to whom he was not married. She was an Indian lady, the equivalent of a wife, and many had loving long term partnerships which would never have been accepted in Britain. Having said that, the army was divided on racial lines. There were British Battalions and Native Battalions and no native could be an officer. This was said to be for security, rather than racial, reasons.

The other obstacle to marriage was that a member of The Company army had to obtain permission to marry. A soldier's wife lived in the barracks and received half a soldier's allowance and their children received a quarter allowance. A wife cost The Company money so in return the wife had to carry out designated tasks. Permission to marry was seldom given to a Gunner and it is noticeable that William, Robert and Michael all married at about the same time as their promotion. Permission to marry was a perk given to NCOs. It seems that either our three wanted to marry so fought for promotion or were promoted so then looked around for a wife.

It seems contradictory to the discouragement of marriage that the Company attempted to solve the problem of a shortage of women by shipping out to India women who may make suitable wives for soldiers and Company employees, although this was becoming less common by 1823. The ladies were given an allowance for a year. They were divided into "gentlewomen" and "other women" and as this cargo was offloaded in Calcutta they would be met by eager suitors, although how a soldier standing on the quayside knew the difference between a gentlewoman and any other is not now known. It was assumed that the women who went to India had failed to find a husband at home. This practice was known as 'The Fishing Fleet' and, if they failed to find a husband in the year they were shipped back, and referred to, rather unkindly, as 'Returned Empties'.

All this may seem remote from the marriages of Our Family but it helps to paint the background picture. It is relevant and will become more relevant later.

Perhaps of closer interest is a very small study of fifty marriages in the same places and within a few weeks of the marriages of Michael

Lally and Mathias Glynn. About 70% of the fifty brides were widows, while 30% of grooms were widowers. Of the spinsters, about 35% were 14 years old, many marrying men old enough to be their fathers. 30% were 15 or 16 years old and the remaining 35% were 17 to 19 years old. Only one spinster was 19 and there were none in the sample over 19 years of age. Many widows were in their teens. The marriage of John Lally, who was not related, was investigated. He married a 15 year old orphan girl and the pages in this Register are full of 14 and 15 year old orphan girls and the witnesses to every marriage were the Master and Mistress of the Allipore Orphan School. They were clearly passing on girls after their government allowance ended when they reached 14. These marriages were not included in the sample of fifty as it would have distorted the results.

What can explain this? We have already looked at the very high death rate, particularly among men. A widow was supported by the Army, with pay and accommodation, for up to six months. What could she do after that? She could not get a job as any native woman could undercut her wages, and where would she live. She had to get married again, and quickly. There are many stories of widows being approached with proposals of marriage at their husband's funeral and of women who married up to eight times. There was no time for mourning. If a newly widowed woman was well accepted by her husband's Company it was considered a matter of honour by the men that they decide who was going to look after her, by marrying her and keeping her military allowance and that for her children. If a wife died, her husband needed to marry quickly so his children were cared for.

The high death rate also produced a large number of orphans. Most towns had an Orphan School, as they were called, which received an allowance for each child until they were 14. After that the boys went into the Army and the girls were married off. Orphanages sometimes held dances and social events to which suitable men were invited, in order to choose a young bride.

This may seem brutal, with little time for love and romance. It was the practicalities that dominated but this was not very different to the situation in London, or Dublin, or Perth where a widow needed a man to support her and a widower needed a woman to look after his children. The difference in India was in the shortage of women and more frequent death.

So, with all this in mind, let's look at William, Robert and Michael, and Thomas and Eliza, and their friend Mathias. It would be nice to think that they were all like we are, with the unimaginable luxuries and privileges of the 21st century West, and that they courted each other, married for love and had families in a 'civilised' way. This may have been the case but, without evidence to the contrary, it must be assumed they followed all the norms of their society. William, Robert and Michael were the younger brothers of Thomas and Eliza and they were all to die early and seeing them go, one by one, must have had a profound effect on Thomas and Eliza.

There must be a degree of uncertainty here due to the lack of official records. Much of this information comes from living descendants and their own family records. As with any description of births, marriages and deaths in other peoples' families, the details can be difficult to follow but study them carefully because the lives of William, Robert and Michael are so typical of life in India at this time.

William Little

It is known that William married Ellen White in 1826 when he was 25 and Ellen was 20. It is not known whether either had been previously married. William and Thomas were both in Fort William at this time so it is very likely that Thomas and Eliza attended the wedding.

William and Ellen had two sons; Michael born in 1828 and William Robert born in about 1831. William Snr died on 2nd August 1830, at the age of 29, in the General Hospital in Fort William. This meant that Ellen was pregnant when he died which may explain why she named the second baby after her late husband's father.

William's widow, Ellen, re-married on 3rd December 1832, more than two years later, to Frederick Crank, a Corporal in The Honourable Company's Engineers who was a bachelor. A witness to her marriage was Mary Little, Robert's wife and this shows that Ellen stayed close to William's family and the two boys' uncles and aunts. Unfortunately, the second son, William Robert, died at about the age of 9, on 2nd February 1840. The elder son, Michael, stayed in India and did well and was a Deputy Magistrate when he died in 1881. He has descendants in America and Australia today.

Robert Little

The next brother was Robert Little who was six years younger than Thomas and he married in about 1829, as usual, in the year that he was promoted. He married Mary, who was a widow and whose maiden name is not known. She was the witness at Ellen Little's marriage to Frederick Crank. Only one of their children is known and he is Robert Thomas, born in 1830. There may have been other children who died in infancy. Our Robert (senior) died at the age of 28, on 7th October 1835 in Fort William. He was a Police Sergeant at the time of his death. Robert Thomas (junior) lived in Calcutta well into old age. He was buried according to the rites of the Roman Catholic Church at the age of 74, on 3rd January 1904. He has descendants today.

Mary, Robert's wife, had at least five husbands. Her marriage to Robert lasted at least six years, the longest of all her husbands. Her husbands were:-

1. John Swiney   1799 – 25th September 1825.
    Date of marriage not known
2. Elias Hunt   1800 – 22nd May 1829.   Date of Marriage 28th February 1826, when Mary was 21, and 5 months after death of Swiney. Two children, Ellen and Lucy.
3. Robert Little   1806 – 7th October 1835   Date of marriage 1829, when Mary was 24 and in the same year as the death of Hunt. One surviving child, Robert Thomas Little.
4. William Dixon   Age and death not known   Date of Marriage, 25th April 1838, when Mary was 33 and 2½ years after death of Little. No known children. Dixon was a Schoolmaster Sergeant
5. Thomas Dadd Brann   1807 – 26th January 1846   Date of marriage, 22nd July 1841, when Mary was 36. Four children Mary Elizabeth, Louisa Esther, Thomas, Adelaide Julia. Brann was a Staff Sergeant.

Mary gave her name as Mary Little at her marriages to both William Dixon and Thomas Dadd Brown so this may mean that her marriage to William Dixon was very brief or this assessment of the records is incorrect.

Michael Lally

Michael was Eliza's brother, about nine years younger than her. He was the last to get married and his short married life follows the pattern described as normal previously, with a complex series of events.

Michael married Sarah Aubril in Fort William on 16th December 1832. He was 26 and she was 14. Her background is not known but the witnesses at their marriage were John and Eliza Ebbs; Eliza being Sarah's sister.

Within two months John Ebbs died and four months later Eliza re-married. The witnesses at Eliza's new marriage were Michael and Sarah Lally.

Two months after this marriage our Michael Lally died. He died on 4th September 1833, nine months after he had married Sarah. There is no record of any children of Michael's marriage but, if there was a child, he or she would have been born after Michael's death.

In September 1836, Sarah, Michael's widow, married again, to William Dudley Salt, a Hospital Apprentice with HM 31st Regiment of Infantry.

Three deaths and more, and each time Thomas and Eliza would have written home to their parents with the sad news. Both fathers were alive and, most likely, Eliza's mother too. Eliza would have been as much a mother as a sister to Michael. In a large family she would have had responsibilities towards her younger siblings from a very early age. No decade or more of childhood for her. Thomas and Eliza must have wondered when it would be their turn to go.

Mathias Glynn

Finally, we come to Mathias Glynn, the friend of the family since their last days in Ireland, and to his importance to our story. Mathias married Mary Doonan in Calcutta on 14th October 1828, in the first year of his promotion to a Barrack Sergeant. Mathias was a 27 year old bachelor and the marriage record states that he was based in Mhow, 1,000 miles (1,600 km) to the west of Calcutta so how he made that journey for the wedding is not known. Perhaps he had been posted back to Calcutta and had not yet taken up his new posting. Mary was a 26 year old widow whose widow's allowance expired at the end of September 1828 so she married just in time. The fact that William Little was a witness at the wedding demonstrates their long term friendship with the Littles.

Mathias and Thomas Little worked together in the same Divisions of the Public Works Department for four years. They would have been posted to different towns and projects together and no doubt their families grew very close as they travelled and lived together. Eliza and Mary would have been present at the births of each other's children. Mary may have been a great comfort to Eliza if, as is suspected, she lost children when they were very young. Mary Glynn had her first child, Maria Elizabeth, on 15th August 1829, ten months after their marriage. Having two Christian names was unusual and one has to wonder whether Mary's choice of Elizabeth as her daughter's second name reflected her closeness to Eliza, whose full Christian name, you will remember, was Elizabeth.

Both Eliza and Mary were expecting again at about the same time in 1831. Eliza Little gave birth to Thomas Jnr. at some time in 1831 and on 15th March 1831 Mary Glynn gave birth to James. But on 27th April, just six weeks later, Mathias was buried. Then, on 31st May, five weeks after that, baby James was buried. What a dreadful time for all of them but then, to add to this disaster, it is also known that Mary Glynn died, perhaps in childbirth.

What was to become of little Maria Elizabeth Glynn who was less than two years old when she was orphaned? The normal course of events was that she would be put in an orphanage with the outcome we have already seen. At 14 Maria would have been got rid of in marriage to any taker when her payments stopped. Thomas and Eliza could not countenance this. Maria was as near to family as possible and Thomas and Eliza adopted her. There would have been no formal record of this but the authorities were probably keen to pass on the responsibility, assuming they even knew. Maria went with Uncle Thomas and Auntie Eliza, to a home she knew and in which she was loved and Eliza then had two babies to look after. Maria became part of the family and travelled to Australia with them later, where she was known as 'the Ward of Thomas Little'.

There may have been other children in the Little family. We know that they lost one, the boy born on board ship, and it is very likely there were more. All we know for certain is that two survived to adulthood, Thomas Jnr and a second son, William, who was born in 1833

This brings us, again, to the obvious question that arises from this study of lives in India and, in particular, the lives of Our Family. The big question must be, how and why did Thomas and Eliza survive when all around them died? Was it just luck; amongst all the statistics some had to survive? There is an answer but first we must remind ourselves of the statistics.

As we have seen, the rate of death in India was enormous. Men died in great numbers if there was a war but also from disease, the heat, accidents or drink. Even murders, often by religious fanatics, duels and fights, more common among an all-male fraternity, and suicides, often due to loneliness, were more common than in Britain. Women lived less violently and could shield themselves from the heat of the day but a major additional cause of their death was childbirth.

Between 1800 and 1850 British mortality in India ran at 69 per thousand per annum, in other words, 690 per thousand over ten years. Wives fared better at 44 per thousand per annum but their children died at a rate of 84 per thousand. No wonder that, in the small sample described earlier, only 8% of deaths were of people over 40 years old. It might be contorting statistics to say that, at 69 per annum, everybody would be dead in 14½ years but it does show that for one man or woman to survive 13½ years in India was rare. For a married couple, Thomas and Eliza, to both survive that time was extraordinary. Was it luck, statistical chance, or was there something different about Thomas and Eliza?

There was something different, but before we look at that there were a few tangible factors. Thomas was not involved in any battles. Early promotion probably meant that he had a non-military or semi-military job from a very early time in India so he was less controlled by the demands for all men to march or train in all conditions, take risks or be closely confined with other men from whom he could catch disease. Thomas didn't spend time with prostitutes, with its high risk of getting disease that could kill him. At a guess, he and Eliza seemed to have had shared ambitions, which put them in a minority. One can imagine Thomas being one to sell his ration of grog to those who wanted double and him saving the money. They certainly had money later. Ambition is a huge motivator. To see a future drives people on. The high rate of suicide in India was often caused by despair, loneliness, pain, asking oneself why life was worth living. Thomas and Eliza did not have these problems. They had each other so they both had the comforts of a home, of sorts, rather than Thomas spending his time drinking or brawling with the lads. There are statistics to prove the benefits of marriage. *On The Population and Mortality in India* (1844) quotes an insurance fund's actuarial assessment of the likelihood of death by any means among single and married soldiers. Single European soldiers were more likely to die, by the following percentages.

Senior Officers	10%	more likely to die if single.
Junior Officers	63%	" " "
All Ranks	38%	" " "

So marriage is a factor in favour of a long life but there was something else almost unique about Thomas and Eliza. They had been together almost since birth and had truly married for love and become one, as the marriage ceremony states.   Each was irreplaceable to the other. That love, care and drive to overcome obstacles, even illness, for the sake of the other is a powerful psychological force. If either was near death, they would be more likely to refuse to accept the inevitability that, like so many around them, it was just their time to go. Someone would have wanted and needed them and one would have cared desperately for the other on their sick bed. What on earth would one have done without the other? If one had died, would the other have just put themselves onto the marriage market for a quick fix. A woman only had the option of a quick marriage to any man, or taking up the offer to military widows of a free passage to Ireland? But by now Ireland wasn't home either.   Did this powerful force of lifetime love, commitment and need, play a part in them being different?

Of course, if one had died we would not be reading this story. It was only the chance of their joint survival that led to a story worth telling. Any story of lives 200 years ago can only be as complete as surviving records allow and 95% of records relate to the 5% of the population who were in the nobility, wealthy and ruling classes. Thomas and Eliza were not in this elite, or not quite. And this brings us to the biggest mystery of all.

How did Thomas and Eliza Little, ordinary, Catholic, Irish folk, who joined the lowest ranks of the army, rise to mix with the highest level of Bengal society and have the money to invest in one of the big enterprises of the day?

INDIA

CHAPTER 8

THE HIGH LIFE

The name of Mr Thomas Little does crop up in surviving records but none describe who or what he was; his work background. So these details of their lives in India must remain unanswered for now. Perhaps when the Bengal newspapers have been digitised and made searchable their names will pop up in the endless columns of small print. In the meantime we can only look there for the big stories of the day so we can envisage the background to Thomas' and Eliza's life and actions.

The major features in the Bengal newspapers of 1837 described efforts to more quickly link India to Britain by sea or over land, the improvement of communications within India, new steam power and opportunities for investment. Other features included actions to mitigate an expected famine and *The Friend of India* campaigned against the sins of slavery in America. Other news was of local businesses, organisations and events.

Descriptions of the new mail service from England best encapsulate the thinking of Thomas' and Eliza's era; the might of the ever-expanding Empire, the great scientific achievements and the business opportunities. If this background picture is to be painted it is worth looking at it in detail. *The Friend of India* was a weekly and therefore contained articles of longer-term significance. On 7th September 1837, just as Thomas' plans to leave for Swan River were progressing, *The Friend of India* heralded the arrival of the mail from Britain to Bombay in just sixty days as a *"fresh triumph"*. It was a new regular monthly mail service. The route was from England to Suez by steam navigation, overland to the Red Sea and, from there, by steam navigation to Bombay. This finally put to rest all other plans including overland through Afghanistan, via steamships on the Euphrates. This 'Euphrates Scheme' had previously been railed against by this newspaper as impractical among *"wild tribes who, for thirty centuries, have been against every man"*. But how long will it be, the paper said, before the steamship continues up the east coast to Calcutta and on to open up new opportunities to British interests in all the eastern seas? Not only was the cost substantially reduced, compared to the long route by sail, but a service by steamship would not be delayed by the vagaries of the weather. The main reason for this new service was to simplify business but the following paragraph from the *Friend of India* in their report also paints, in a typically grand effusive tone, a more personal picture and a dramatic comparison with our life today.

"It is impossible to contemplate the establishment of steam communication, as now arranged on a solid and permanent basis, without feeling the mind overpowered by sensations to which residents in India have hitherto been strangers. To commercial transactions it must necessarily impart a character of more certainty, at the same time as it infuses new life and vigour into them. To the movements of governments it will give that confidence which the opportunity of so speedy a reference to the seat of authority must necessarily bring with it. But it is as men with social ties, rather than as merchants and politicians, that we would dwell upon the blessing now conferred upon us. Our connections, often our dearest connections, are in our native land and thither do our warm affections tend. We now have the high gratification of enjoying intercourse with them by letter every month and of being able to send or to receive replies in the brief space of five months. The distance that separates us seems all but annihilated, our affectionate recollections will be constantly nourished with fresh impulses. It appears, indeed, as if the bonds that bind us to our native land have become, all at once, multiplied and immeasurably strengthened. The feeling of dreary exile from home which oppressed the mind in India is removed and all the generous sympathies of the soul will appear to have acquired a new elasticity."

Some of the Illustrated London News pictures of the passage of the Indian Mail. Arriving at Marseilles, crowds gathering to watch the spectacle at Folkestone, signalling the ship's approach, unloading at low tide.

Over the following few years this revolutionary mail service became an international sensation. It became a relay race, a challenge to get the mail delivered more quickly, eagerly anticipated each month. On 6th July 1844, the *Illustrated London News* carried an article on the wonders of the regular mail service and confirmed that it had spread eastwards as had been envisaged at its inception. This article too was full of the greatness of technical advances and beneficial growth of the British Empire which dominated the world and on which the sun never set.

> *"(The subject of the Indian Mail) has grown to be one of greater importance as the states of Hindostan have become essential to the welfare of the home country; China has been added to our commercial empire; and the course of trading adventure on the coasts of Burmah, Japan and many wonderous places of the orient seas have combined to give all Post Office arrangements with these immense territories a degree of surpassing interest. The flight of the Indian Mail is, in truth, a wonder of the day. Thousands follow its course for pleasure or instruction and even the governor General, throwing off the customary solemnity of a state march, has at last decided to take the post passage to Calcutta.*

By 1844 the mail from all the eastern empire was collected in Bombay. It then progressed in sealed steel trunks to Suez by steam ship and across the desert on wagons to Alexandria. From here the mail ship went to Marseilles to refuel. While the mail ship sped on through the Straits of Gibraltar, vital mail and abstracts of news reports and government papers went overland by a 24 hour relay of horses and drivers, via Paris, to Boulogne. At every stage its arrival was heralded by the telegraph so that not a minute should be wasted. At Boulogne the ship, in full steam and ready to go, headed for Folkestone. If it arrived at high tide it could sail straight into the harbour. At low tide skiffs were sent out to take the precious trunks. In bad weather fishing boats were sent out; their crews being used to unloading goods in high seas. A four-horse fast coach took the trunks to a special express train bound for London where men waited at their desks for a post runner to deliver the mail, hopefully in another record time.

There was an excitement about the success of all this, felt in London and by Thomas and his associates in Calcutta, who we shall soon meet.

The improvement of communications within India was equally important. Progress was reported on the metalling of the Grand Trunk Road which would eventually reach Kabul. The wonders of the four new steamships plying the Ganges were described in detail in the issue of 15th June. Such was their success that five more were ordered with exciting plans to navigate further upstream and on other rivers to the north and west. The engines came out from Britain and the ships were made in Bengal. Very soon there would be freight cargoes once a week and passengers every two weeks. Even newspapers from around the world were making their way speedily to remote stations. Journeys that took a month would now be completed in a week.

Business was at the core of life in India. Britain was amassing great wealth from the industrial revolution gathering pace in her homeland and there were not enough opportunities to invest that money at home. Potential investors shunned investment in nearby European countries due to bureaucracy, language and currency difficulties, and the insecurity of company and financial law. Also, from 1803 to 1815, which was in recent memory, Britain had been at war with Napoleon's France, notably at Trafalgar, the Peninsula Wars and finally Waterloo. Britain was isolated from its warring European neighbours, particularly due to Napoleon's Berlin Decree of 1806 which forbade the nations under his control from trading with Britain. Britain retaliated by blockading European ports for eight years. None of this was conducive to trade with Europe. One outcome of these years of turmoil was that Britain looked out to the world where it now dominated the seas and quickly developed into the world's greatest economic power. British investors looked to the Empire, governed by law with which they were familiar, security of tenure, a common language, currency and customs. Likewise, businessmen in India were looking for new opportunities and these were widely reported and advertised in the local press. Indian society contained many risk-takers and adventurers; an obvious fact perhaps, bearing in mind that many had left England 'to make their fortune'. This was the atmosphere in Calcutta – to create their own industrial revolution in Bengal.

Many of these entrepreneurs entered India as employees of The East India Company or as officers in its army. The Company was flexible enough to permit them to have jobs and make investments alongside their main employment. They used their salary or money from home to build up businesses, many eventually being successful enough to leave the Company's employ entirely. Thomas was not an officer but it is most likely that he followed this route, even if it was at a lower level than most.

One of these risk takers and adventurers, at the top of Bengal society, was Charles Robert Prinsep and it was he who, can we say, took Thomas Little under his wing. The Prinsep family was dominant in Bengal society and business from the 1820s. There were eight Prinsep brothers who had successful business interests throughout the world but principally in India. After John Prinsep died in Angostura in Venezuela in 1819, Charles Robert became the oldest brother. He was born in England in 1789, his father having made his fortune in India. In 1824 Charles qualified as a Doctor of Law in London and promptly went to Calcutta where he was appointed Standing Legal Counsel to the East India Company. In this high position he was responsible for all legal representation of the Company, of which there was plenty. Later he was to become Advocate General of Bengal

From 1824 to 1830 six Prinsep brothers were in Bengal and had stakes in nearly every commercial opportunity. Among the brothers were the Assay Master at the Calcutta Mint, the architect of the new city of Benares, a pioneer of steam ships on the River Ganges. They were in business in shipping, indigo, silk and cotton trading, nutmeg growing, salt refining and newspaper publishing, among many others. They built canals and were involved in other public works. One brother was an authority on ancient Indian history. Charles was perhaps the most successful and was said to have legendary wealth, living in one of the greatest mansions in Bengal, known as Belvedere, which later became the Lieutenant Governor's residence and now houses the National Library of Bengal. William Prinsep was an accomplished artist whose illustrations appear opposite and elsewhere. These two paintings Of Charles Prinsep's house were completed by William Prinsep in the mid 1830s, just as Thomas was becoming involved with Charles Prinsep and may have visited this house.

Belvedere, the home of Charles Prinsep, which Thomas may have visited on business or socially. *British Library*

The gardens of Belvedere, sloping down to the Hooghly River. A small boy is shaded by a servant as he admires the ships. *British Library*

From his arrival in Bengal in 1824 or 1825 Charles Prinsep showed particular interest in Australia which was just beginning to be attractive to investors. Remember that it was only twenty-one years previously, in 1803, that Australia had been circumnavigated. It was only in 1824 that the British Admiralty officially changed the name of the continent to 'Australia' rather than Terra Australis or New Holland as used before. The new Provinces of Australia were tiny and still being formed during this period. Britain was discovering the world and opening it to new trade opportunities and Australia was an exciting new land, ripe for investment. The British in India saw the new continent almost as an extension of India, in the same way that Singapore, Straits Settlements, Penang and other small colonies were, spread across the ocean.

In 1828 Charles Prinsep made his first venture into Australia by acquiring land in Van Diemen's Land (now Tasmania). He sent Captain Michael Fenton there as his agent and stocked the estate, named Adelphi, with cattle and horses.

His second Australian venture, of 1830, ended in tragedy. Prinsep's ship carrying his agent, workers and all their livestock and equipment was lost at sea. It vanished without trace somewhere in the Indian Ocean.

His third Australian venture, of mid 1837, was the setting up of the Bengal Australian Association and in this he was not alone. There were 39 investors in this company, including Thomas Little. Perhaps inspired by the new regular monthly mail service from Britain the aim was to set up a regular monthly shipping service to the various Australian colonies. It would operate like a bus, calling at Swan River, King George's Sound (Albany), Kangaroo Island (off Adelaide), Hobart Town or Launceston and terminate at Sydney. And then return. As a priority the ships would carry passengers in superior accommodation and mail. Goods were to be a lower priority. The Association's strategy was not only to run a profitable shipping line but to encourage trade and be in at its inception. The Association also publicised the health attractions of the Australian climate. People resident in India who had long term health problems would go to Cape Town or home to England to recuperate and Australia was promoted as a nearby healthy alternative.

The Bengal Australian Association had a committee of four, including Charles Prinsep. It had 35 other subscribers. In total they had invested in 76 shares of 500 Rupees each. This is where we find Thomas Little listed among the great men of Bengal, as a subscriber or shareholder. All these men were in business or in a profession in Bengal. As well as Charles Prinsep, who we know, here are a few of them.

- Dwarakanath Tagore was probably the highest ranking Indian civilian in Bengal society and commerce. He was a western educated Bengali Brahmin with vast landholdings and interests in shipping, banking and insurance. He was a business partner with many British men in jute mills, coal mines and tea plantations. He founded the Union Bank of Calcutta. If you remember, it was one of his mansions that Thomas had marched past on his first day on Indian soil.

- Edward Stirling was a senior member of the Indian civil service. His brother was James Stirling the naval explorer. James was the first Briton to explore the Swan River and first Governor of Western Australia. Edward had, in 1835, written a book on Persia and the other states through which Russia would need to march an army if they were to invade India – an important topical subject.

- Ross Donnelly Mangles was Eton educated and a member of the British parliament. He was Deputy Lieutenant of London and a director of the New Zealand Company. In 1857 he was to become Chairman of the East India Company. He was an author of Christian books and one on the duties of colonial governments.

- J P Mackilligin was to become Chairman of the India Steam Navigation Company and director of the New Oriental Life Insurance Society.

- N Paliologus was an Attorney and Notary Public.

- J W Alexander was Assistant to the Accountant General of Bengal. He established the Bengal Bonded Warehouse Association. He was on the committee of the Calcutta Christian School Book Society.

- R W Allen was Secretary of the Union River Insurance Company and on the Committee of the Bengal Catholic Orphanage.

These are just scraps of biographies listed to describe some of the people with whom Thomas was now mixing. They were highly educated, successful and wealthy men. How had Thomas risen to these heights? How had he amassed enough money to invest in this company, and maybe others? He was still nominally just a soldier in The Company Army. If Thomas had one 500 Rupee share it was the equivalent of £64 which equals about £6400 today. That is a lot of money in a country where everything was so cheap. The sum of the 76 shares would have been about enough to buy a good second hand ocean going ship.

Yet in 1837 Thomas decided to leave his new, elevated position in society and he and Eliza and their family were to, again, embark on completely new life. He took employment as the agent of Charles Prinsep, to go to the Swan River Colony, as it was still referred to, and to buy land on his behalf with the prime purpose of breeding horses for the Indian market. It was only eight years since the western side of Australia had been claimed by the British crown and the settlement at Perth had been established. In 1837 the British population of this vast area was only about 2,000, spread mainly along the coast in tiny groups and individual homesteads. Thomas and Eliza were to abandon all they had achieved in Bengal and the benefits, lifestyle and status they had won and start again. Why?

Ambition is a great driver and must have played a large part in Thomas' decision. Here was an opportunity to be in at the beginning of a grand project, a new colony. Australia's climate was much better than that in India where Thomas and Eliza had seen the deaths of their brothers and several children. Thomas, once there, would be largely his own boss, at least three months away in return communication, with Charles Prinsep. He must have imagined that, as in Bengal, he could develop his own business interests alongside his responsibilities to his employer and become truly his own man. There must have been an element of Thomas being in awe of the great man, Charles Prinsep, and being flattered by the trust and responsibility that Prinsep was placing on him.

This says a lot about Thomas. Charles Prinsep was no fool and he was entrusting Thomas with a large amount of money to spend wisely on his behalf, without being able to confirm his actions beforehand. Freemasonry was very prominent in India and it is likely that Thomas was a Mason. The Prinseps were Masons and the honour among this fraternity is likely to be a factor in this trust. Prinsep also thought Thomas capable of carving a successful business, physically out of the bare earth of an unknown land; to buy and sell, employ, feed and build, and to breed quality horses. Clearly Thomas was reliable, trustworthy and skilled. But what were his skills? In the years prior to 1837, when we know little about him, Thomas must have successfully managed operations in Bengal and presumably proved his ability to breed animals, if not horses.

These were all positive reasons to go but there were great risks too. In these early days, who knew how this new land of Australia would thrive, or not? The weighing of the opportunities against the risks must have produced a positive result. However, there was also something driving Thomas and Eliza <u>away</u> from the opportunities that presented themselves in Bengal. This can be found in the list of shareholders in the Bengal Australian Association.

Class and status were very important in British and Indian society. As we have seen, they were much more important than race. There were several Indian gentlemen on the list of shareholders. In all documents, reports or newspapers everybody's name was always prefixed or suffixed with their status; Lord, Colonel or Esquire, etc. So let's look at the 39 Subscribers to the Bengal Australian Association. They comprised:-

Indian dancers entertain Europeans in a grand house during the Hindu festival of Durga Puja. William Prinsep, mid 1830s

- 30 men entitled Esquire (Esq). This was a complimentary rank given to men of noble birth, members of the landed gentry (owning c.1000+ acres of land), men of high rank in the civil service or who had achieved distinction in other spheres.
- 5 men with military rank; 2 Colonels, 2 Captains, 1 Lieutenant. To have bought your commission must mean you are from a family of high status.
- 3 Baboos. This title intimated a learned and respected Hindu gentleman, not Indian nobility. The equivalent, or higher, than the English Esquire.
- 1 plain Mr. A man with no rank or status

There were no Lords or other nobility. These were all self-made entrepreneurs, the sort of men who, uniquely in Britain, created the industrial revolution and who particularly thrived in the Indian environment. But there was only one man singled out, not deliberately or maliciously but just according to form, as a plain Mr. He was Mr. Thomas Little.

Thomas knew where he stood and knew that he had reached the limit, or beyond, of his rise in India. He and Eliza may have learnt the manners, language, etiquette and social graces of the upper class but this could not hide their humble background and the stigma attached to it. In Australia Thomas could be free of this, a large fish in a small pond.

We cannot move on without picking up on and emphasising a key point in the previous paragraph. If Thomas had successfully made his way into the upper circles of Bengal business and social life he would have needed a wife who could mix as freely with the wives of Thomas' great associates in their social milieu. No fourteen year old orphan or rough soldier's widow could have pulled this off. Surely, Eliza must have matched Thomas in acquired social graces, educated conversation, style, and ambition.

In readiness for his new adventure, Thomas left The Company Army on 10th October 1837 after serving just thirteen years of his eighteen year contract. He would have had to get permission to buy himself out but, with supporters like Charles Prinsep, this would not have presented a problem.

The Bengal Australian Association planned their first sailing to be in November 1837 and bought their first ship – or thought they had. She was an ocean-going barque of 500 tons but it transpired at the last moment that the man they were buying her from had defaulted on payments and the mortgagee had taken the ship in lieu of payment and was sending her back to England. In great urgency, all they could get hold of was *Gaillardon*, a barque of only 391 tons; small by ocean going standards. She would have been about 100 feet long and 25 feet wide, about the size of the singles area on a tennis court. She also needed considerable work to provide passenger cabins in the poop and below decks. This work was completed and she set sail a few weeks later than planned, on 16th December 1837, crammed with passengers, animals and cargo – not quite to the standard they had claimed in the company's prospectus but it was a start.

Gaillardon was less than a third of the size of *Macqueen*, on which Thomas and Eliza had made their last sea voyage and we do not have the benefit of a ship's log. But we can be quite precise in what was loaded, partly from reports in Calcutta but mainly from reports in the Swan River newspapers for which the arrival of any ship was newsworthy.

Gaillardon's Captain was an Englishman, James Rapson and the crew was Indian lascars, semi-military sailors. Any ship, even a small one, would need at least forty crew. There were about sixty passengers, including the Littles and their Indian servants. James Milne was to act as Thomas' manager, and 23 Indian hill coolies were to work for Thomas in Australia. Six of the coolies had wives. There were another ten Englishmen and a Chinaman and also on board were eighteen military convicts being taken to the penal colony in Tasmania. So, one hundred souls sailed together.

Animals included "several" Indian water buffaloes for Thomas' agricultural work and probably some horses, as well as the chickens and sheep for food on the voyage and to establish a food supply in their new home. It can't have been easy to load large animals like buffaloes (and unload them) as Calcutta port had very few facilities for ships to go alongside docks. Most loading was done on barges and 'flats' which, as their name suggests, were floating platforms often pulled back and forth from ship to shore by ropes, the ship being moored off-shore.

Cargo would have been the mail plus everything that Thomas and Eliza would need to set up home and business in a new land where very little, except perhaps wooden furniture, was readily available. This may have included a cast iron kitchen range for cooking, pots and pans, cutlery and crockery, and the family's personal items; clothes, books, etc. All the tools and ironmongery needed to build houses and barns would be on board and ploughs and fencing equipment if horses were to be bred. There may have been bricks and mortar for chimneys and even wagons on deck so the buffaloes could pull everything to a chosen site. There was food, rice and ghee are mentioned, for the voyage and self-sufficiency beyond that. And drinking water, of course. There was also other cargo for Swan River and all the other ports of call around Australia.

Imagine all these people, animals and cargo squeezed onto a tennis court and you can see how crammed life on *Gaillardon* was to be. The ship was packed. But the senior passengers on *Gaillardon* were Thomas and Eliza Little, their two boys, Thomas and William, and Maria Glynn. Unlike the voyage of *Macqueen* when Thomas and Eliza were shut below nearly all of the time, they were now accommodated in the main cabin which was private, spacious for its day, on deck and with windows. They dined with the captain. Thomas must have known the fate of Charles Prinsep's previous ship of 1830, but he accepted that travel was a risky business, as was life itself. They travelled with hope and confidence again to a new life.

WESTERN AUSTRALIA

CHAPTER 9

ARRIVAL

Thomas and Eliza's journey took them across 4,500 miles (7,200km) of open ocean and for weeks they would not have sighted land or, in that part of the world, another ship. They were alone and totally out of communication. Their tiny vessel was at the mercy of the wind and waves, with days of peace and tranquility, interspersed by days of noise, frantic activity and probably fear. Guided only by the stars, they were heading for a tiny speck of human habitation on the edge of vast new continent, nearly twice the size of the whole of the India they had left behind. On Australia there were just a few individual British settlements and it was only ten years previously that the whole continent had been claimed by Britain and eight years since the Swan River Colony, to which they were heading, was established. It was to be another 26 years before the States took on a form similar to that we recognise today, although they were to remain separate colonies for another 63 years. There was no long history to tell you about. As far as the British settlers were concerned, there was no great civilisation to confront, as in India, but just a very few primitive nomadic people of little consequence. Thomas, Eliza and their family were heading for a new land and a new life of risks, opportunities and surprises.

Gaillardon arrived safely in Fremantle on the Swan River, on 4th February 1838 after 49 days - 7 weeks - at sea. Thomas was 39 and Eliza 41 so, by the standards of the day, they were not young people but, nevertheless, they were eager to start a new life. Their two boys, Thomas Jnr and William were about 7 and 5 years old. Maria Glynn, who had been part of the family for 6½ years, was 8½ years old.

Notification of the arrival of Gaillardon in the Perth Gazette and Western Australian Journal. All the ships at anchorage were listed as it was a matter of great interest.

The description recorded by J T Reilly of his arrival at the same place helps us to imagine the Littles' arrival. Even though Reilly's arrival was thirteen years later, the scene would have been much the same. Reilly's journey had taken six months from Tilbury, east of London, including a week at the Isle of Wight, off southern England, to pick up 29 Parkhurst Boys, and a week at Cape Town. Parkhurst Boys were criminals sentenced to deportation but under the age of 15 and considered to have been reformed. Their age and reformed character meant that they were strictly not to be classed as convicts.

Six months on board a sailing vessel is enough to exhaust the patience of every landsman and the desire to tread terra firma once more becomes an exquisite sensation. Landing in Fremantle in 1851 was conducted in a very primitive fashion. Men, women, children and luggage were passed over the ship's side into open boats and when these were full were pushed off amid the farewell cheers of the occupants. . . . . On reaching Fremantle the women were carried ashore while the boys had to jump and wade ashore. The order to jump ashore was promptly obeyed and in a very short time some forty boys and girls were rollicking on the beach, pleased and delighted at having reached their new home.

The Little boys and Maria would surely have rollicked on the beach in just the same manner, then the whole family would have gone off to some good accommodation leaving the unloading of their cargo to others. The Indian water buffalo would have created much interest and maybe some problems in getting them ashore but cows, horses and even carts had all been managed before.

Certainly, The Littles would have dined with James Stirling, the Governor of Western Australia on their arrival. Stirling's brother was, like Thomas, a shareholder in the Bengal Australian Association. His sister was married to Ross Mangles, also a shareholder, prominent in the East India Company and later to be its Chairman. These great families were intertwined in such ways, so for these personal reasons and for the development of the Colony, the Governor would have been keen to give Thomas Little every assistance.

The Littles stayed in Perth, 15 miles (24km) from where they landed, until July 1837. Then they sailed from Safety Bay, 20 miles (32km) south of Fremantle, to Port Leschenault (now called Bunbury), a further 80 miles (130km) down the coast in the local ship, *Lady Stirling*. They arrived safely despite concern for them after a severe storm blew up after they had left; such storms being frequent during the winter months. These so-called ports spread down the coast were tiny, no more than a safe mooring from where passengers and goods were ferried ashore in rowing boats. Lady Stirling had been built in Fremantle just two years previously and was a cutter of only 25 tons. The fact that she was wrecked just two years later in a similar journey down the coast when she sprang a leak illustrates the precarious nature of life at that time. Shipwrecks along that coast were not infrequent but they did supply useful material for settlers, such as timber, ironwork and implements ranging from saucepans to winches.

On arrival at their final destination the family lived at Picton, a little inland from Bunbury, in tents they had brought with them. Only a couple of other settlers lived at Picton so they were immediately dependent on their own resources and supplies that they would have accumulated during their months in Perth. The buffaloes, wagons and heavy supplies would have come overland. This land around Picton was part of a grant held by the Governor, Sir James Stirling, and this could be a reason why Thomas chose to settle here. Stirling would have wanted to help Prinsep. Thomas would have been making enquiries about land that was available and would have been aware that the best land had already been granted to landowners in large plots by the government on condition that they started to develop them within ten years. If they did not develop the land or if they abandoned it, the land would revert to the Crown and become available again in 1840 or 1841. This could have been another reason why Stirling encouraged Thomas to live on his land. It would have been to Stirling's advantage as Thomas would make improvements which were necessary if Stirling was to be granted permanent ownership of the land. Many plots would become available if they were not developed, due mainly to a shortage of labour and capital, so Thomas could bide his time. By bringing his own labour with him, Thomas would develop the land promptly and he was also entrusted with Prinsep's letters of credit to the value of £5,000. This enormous sum was plenty to buy large areas of good land and maintain his family and workforce until the operation created an income. Thomas was very well placed.

His first purchase for Charles Prinsep was 1,832 acres of the Leschenault Peninsula, running north to south down the coast. It consisted mainly of sand dunes so most of it was not suitable for crops. This was probably why nobody else had taken it up but it would be suitable for his purpose of breeding of horses. It was bounded on three sides by water so only needed to be fenced across the narrow neck of the peninsula. The easiest access to it was across the water which could be better than cutting new tracks to Bunbury and other settlements inland. It was on the coast and near a sheltered harbour so was ideal for trade by sea. The shallow, warm inlet behind the peninsula was full of fish which were easy to catch and there was a multitude of water birds, some of which were worth catching to eat.

It was over a year before the Little family and staff all moved over the estuary to the new property which Thomas had built. It was a substantial, high quality timber building, named Belvidere after Prinsep's massive palace in Calcutta, called Belvedere with different spelling. Wood and bark houses were built for the workers and paddocks were fenced off ready for the first horses. Visitors had to shout across the water and, unless there was a strong wind blowing, their call would be heard and result in a boat coming over to collect them. Horses and cattle were waded and swum across as the water wasn't deep.

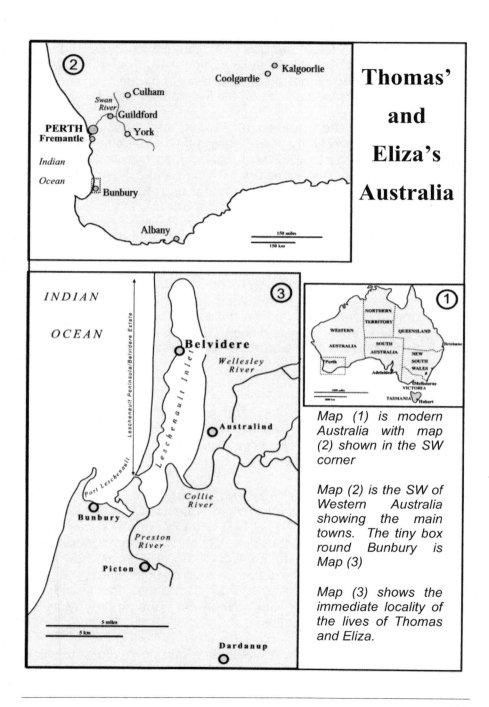

Thomas' and Eliza's Australia

Map (1) is modern Australia with map (2) shown in the SW corner

Map (2) is the SW of Western Australia showing the main towns. The tiny box round Bunbury is Map (3)

Map (3) shows the immediate locality of the lives of Thomas and Eliza.

Several of the estates nearby were being taken up by British men who brought their families with them. There was great social interaction between these families. We shall concentrate on two of them, the Cliftons and Wollastons, who arrived after the Littles moved to Belvidere. From these two families came four surviving diaries which shed glorious light on the lives of our Little family.

Marshall Waller Clifton, known as Waller, had been tempted to emigrate by the opportunity of overseeing the development of a vast estate of 103,000 acres (162 sq miles) owned by a consortium of British businessmen and investors. It was named Australind in the hope of encouraging trade between India and Australia. The plan was that Waller Clifton would sell and let out the estate in lots and build a central township on the lines of an English village with the dream of becoming a sort of lord of the manor. He arrived in 1841 with his wife, six sons and six daughters, and many workers from Britain. Three more ship loads of settlers with capital and workers joined them later. But there were many doubters right from the beginning who said the scheme would never work, perhaps due to the strange structure of the company as well as the poor quality of the land and the economic conditions. Even in its first year, in 1841, Rev John Smithies of the Swan River Methodist Mission wrote to his sponsors in London:-

> *If any of your friends are thinking of Australind as a point of emigration tell them to Stop. It is one of the greatest **puffs** that there has been for some time. I should be sorry if any of our Methodist friends or others should be so deluded as to embark for such a place.*

Waller Clifton was 54 when he arrived, having been Secretary to the Victualling Board for the Royal Navy in London. He was a member of the Royal Society. His family had been living in France for four years before they came to the Swan River Settlement. Waller and his eldest daughter, Louisa, kept diaries which show how they, particularly his sophisticated daughters, had some difficulty getting used to the very primitive life that confronted them and the characters they had to mix with. When they arrived they received great assistance from the Littles.

The second family was the Wollastons. Rev. John Wollaston was an Anglican priest and he arrived with his wife Mary and six children, also in 1841 when the Littles had been at Belvidere for two or three years. Rev. Wollaston was 50 years old and the children were between 6 and 20. The Wollastons left a genteel, domestic and social life as vicar of a rural parish in Cambridgeshire. Rev. Wollaston left England believing he had been appointed Chaplain to the Australind community, only to find on arrival that this was not the case and that he was without a stipend and extremely short of money. Also, according to the memoire of Mrs Mary Wollaston, they arrived woefully unprepared and the following brief description of their first year illustrates the harsh life even the Littles may have had to endure at times.

The Wollastons only had a brief stay in Fremantle and on arrival in Bunbury in May 1841 spent their first night on the beach exposed to the first of the winter gales. It was to be three months before the prefabricated wooden house they had brought with them from England arrived from Fremantle. On their first day, according to "God's providence", as Mary Wollaston wrote, they received two

An artist's impression of Belvidere, Thomas and Eliza's home from 1838 to 1854. It was drawn by Henry Prinsep after the Littles had moved out but must be a good representation of what the house and surrounding land was like in their time. The trees are reflecting in the water of the inlet.

offers.   One was to stay temporarily in the house of Henry Ommanney. The other was an opportunity to purchase 115 acres of land of which 5 acres was an established vegetable garden and orchard. This was bought from Captain Coffin, an American whaler who was anxious to return to America. He lived on his land in a series of huts he had made from the wreckage of one of his whaling ships. Mary Wollaston, who was very fragile physically and of a nervous disposition, had set out from England with two maids but one was dismissed for insolence at Cape Town and the other went off on her own at Fremantle. They seemed to have brought no other servants or workers with them and had great difficulty finding any. It took a week for the family to clean Coffin's huts so they could move in but even after this they must have been very different from the vicarage in Cambridgeshire.   They suffered a year or more of deprivation and hard work, doing things like washing, cooking and mending clothes that they had not been used to doing before. Their meals consisted mainly of rice, boiled onions and bread. Mary lists the meat they ate which included fish of all sorts, emu, possum, bandicoot, rat, crows, pigeons, ducks and quails, all caught in hunting trips by their boys.

In the face of all their problems, Thomas went out of his way to help by shipping some of his men, equipment and oxen over the estuary to help the Wollastons get established quickly at Picton. They all became good friends despite their great religious differences. It was at the Wollastons that Thomas, Eliza and their three children dined just before they returned to India for, what was said to be, an extended holiday, in 1842. The visit was noted in John Wollaston's diary.

Friday 11th March 1842: Mr & Mrs Little and their three young people came by appointment and lunched (I killed and dressed a nice chicken) and took leave of us previous to their embarking for India, whither they are going we hope only for a time. They went up to Fremantle in a schooner. They are very nice people, though Papists, and have been very kind to poor Dr. Carpenter, fetching him across the estuary to their house in order that they might nurse him better than he got nursed at Australind. They have left him at Belvidere under the care of Mr Onslow, with Dr. Green (but a sad and incorrigible drunk) brought from The Vasse to attend him.

It was announced in the newspapers in March 1842, as all these things were, that Thomas Little was returning to India on business and taking his family on an extended holiday. No doubt Eliza had old friends she could visit in Calcutta and would appreciate a bit of the luxury of British India. The truth was, as the Wollastons probably knew, that they may never return as after four years hard work at Belvidere, the estate was still not bringing good returns. Their trip was to discuss the future with Charles Prinsep. Was this a pre-planned five-year review or was Thomas summoned to explain himself? The Littles were gone for a year so must have spent six to eight months in India and the fact that the whole family went suggests that remaining there was a possibility. They had plenty of time to weigh the benefits and decided to return to Australia. They returned in March 1843, and Thomas was still employed by Charles Prinsep who had weighed the benefits too and still had confidence in Thomas.

Louisa Clifton's watercolour of Koombana Bay looking across to the Littles' land on the Leschenault Peninsular. It shows the character of the surrounding landscape.

WESTERN AUSTRALIA

CHAPTER 10

COLONNIAL LIFE

Their year's absence, from March 1842 to March 1843, after four years in Western Australia, gives us time to look at the political and economic background of the early years of the new colony, of which Thomas and Eliza and the children were to play important parts. This was the background of their social lives too, in a tiny colony, not much bigger than a 21st century village, where everybody must have known everybody else. Yet it had a Governor, post service, societies, several newspapers, hotels and shops which must have been like nothing we know today. Over the years of Thomas' and Eliza's lives the colony developed greatly but it remained small and isolated compared with other parts of Australia.

The Swan River Settlement had been officially claimed for Britain in 1829, only nine years before the Littles' arrival. A census taken two years after their arrival, in 1840, showed the British population for the whole vast area of Western Australia to be only 2,354. This was made up of 1,205 men, 557 women and 592 children.

Jumping ahead for a moment to 1848, another census of Western Australia gave the total British population as still only 4,622. This consisted of 2,818 males and 1,804 females. The colony was not growing quickly. The 'Aboriginal Native population' was estimated at an additional 1,960, of which 541 were 'casually or regularly employed by colonists'. Populations of the largest towns in 1848 were as follows, Bunbury being the fifth largest:-

Perth	1148
Fremantle	426
Albany	173
Guildford	95
Bunbury	66
Rest of WA	2714

These towns are shown on the map on page 123. Perth, Fremantle and Guildford were within 20 miles (30km) of each other on the Swan River. So the population of the Colony was tiny and these people were spread over hundreds of square miles. As we have seen, the Little's ultimate destination was a hundred miles (160km) south of the two main towns of Perth and Fremantle near the hamlet of Bunbury with forty or fifty inhabitants at that time, with a similar number living in isolated holdings scattered in the surrounding countryside.

The Littles were wise to have brought their own workers and servants with them because of the great shortage of manual labour in Western Australia. This shortage was a key factor that hindered the development of the Colony as so much of the early work was manual; clearing the bush, putting up buildings and fences, laying down roads, planting and harvesting crops. India had an unlimited supply of cheap, willing labour which was absent in Western Australia and the Littles had been well advised to bring labourers with them, and domestic servants too. It was a condition of being granted land that the owner brought his workers with him – or substantial capital. This was not uncommon in new colonies, surrounded by land waiting to be cultivated. In fact, just as the Littles had arrived the Colonial Government was drawing up plans (in May 1838) to actively encourage the immigration of workers, particularly young apprentices to learn a trade. Bringing their own staff with them demonstrates just how far Thomas and Eliza had progressed since Ireland and those early days in Bengal.

There were two main reasons for the shortage of labour. Firstly, it may be thought that the aborigines would be a good supply of labour but there were so few of them and the colonists did not consider them to be reliable workers, as Indian natives were. The aborigines had no idea of time or the need to work, in the European sense, so came and went as they pleased. They had no idea of property so walked off with things that caught their eye. Although some learnt to communicate in English they were considered difficult to educate as they didn't have the concentration or see the need for it. Of course, the aborigines saw things very differently as they had their own culture which was suddenly being taken from them. Why should they abandon their traditional culture for something alien? This was the first generation of aborigine to witness the arrival of the white man and his strange ways and they had only recently, in the mid 1830s, been violently subjugated by them. The aborigines were nomads whose land and hunting grounds were being stolen from them. Their lives and society did have a structure but now they were punished for doing things they had always done, on their own lands and by a set of laws that were foreign to them. For example, their lands were being fenced in by the newcomers. The aborigines used fire to hunt out animals and to regenerate the grass but this was often seen as dangerous aggression by the colonists.

A small story illustrates the remoteness of the population and the attitude of the aborigines and is included because it involves the Littles. The Sisters of Mercy, who we will hear about later, needed to send an urgent message to Thomas Little and the quickest way was to send an aborigine who worked for them. The journey, on foot, would take him five days and he would only go if the Sisters allowed his wife and daughter to live in the Convent while he was away. He was afraid that somebody would steal them and after five days he may not be able to track them through the bush to get them back.

The second reason for the shortage of manual workers was that there were no convicts in Western Australia at this time. Western Australia was different from the other Australian colonies that had been built over many previous years by convict labour and immigration of less-skilled British people. Western Australia was founded as a so-called 'Free Colony' in which large tracts of land were allocated and sold to investors to make a good return and in which market forces would control things like the supply of labour. These investors did not expect to do the work themselves. In the

Perth from Mount Eliza, drawn in 1856 for the Illustrated London News

Fremantle drawn in 1857 for the Illustrated London News.
These two sketches show just how small these towns were, even 20 years
after Thomas and Eliza arrived,

other colonies convict labour built the infra-structure and poor British immigrants, many on assisted passages, and ex-convicts would work the land or act as servants in the reasonable hope that they could eventually buy their own plot, make a good living and be their own master. Owning your own small plot was not as easy in Western Australia as most land had been allocated in the vast grants to people who wanted to perpetuate the landlord system of England and Ireland.

The lack of labour, the style of land ownership and the small size of the local market gave Western Australia a number of problems that would hinder its development. Some of the land was of poor quality. A farmer, having cleared the trees and scrub and having had a few good years, could find the weather dry for a couple of years. Then, not only would crops fail but the soil would turn to dust and blow away. The soil was sandy and saline in places and lacking in nutrients so cattle and sheep were susceptible to various incurable diseases, notably coastee disease.

The vastness of the land, the lack of people and lack of trade with the outside world gave the colony of Western Australia a lonely remoteness, demonstrated by the fact that *Gaillardon* was one of only fourteen ocean going ships to call at Swan River in 1838. And, of course, the timing of arrivals could never be exact as even the short sailing time from India, compared with that from Britain, could vary by weeks due to weather. Arrivals and departures by sea, of people and freight, were published in the local papers to an interested audience. Ships brought people, news and goods for sale and the scattered populace always wanted to be informed. Word had got round back in the home country that Western Australia was remote, arid and risky and most emigrants would choose a better established colony with a better chance of success. Charles Prinsep and his Bengal Australian Association saw this remoteness as temporary and lack of development as a business opportunity. And land was very cheap. And it was weeks closer to India. To maximise the value of their investments they had to overcome this remoteness, so the Association's plan was to improve trade links and encourage immigration through regular shipping. It was Prinsep, personally, who by sending Thomas, demonstrated his confidence in this opportunity.

The interior of Western Australia from the Illustrated London News of 1857.
The top sketch shows Culham, 60 miles (100km) NE of Perth in the Upper
Swan Valley. Only the residence of S P Phillips Esq existed there then.

York, 60 miles (100km) east of Perth in 1857

Remoteness, small size of the population, lack of labour, poor land in places; these were problems upon which everybody agreed. There was another problem upon which there was great disagreement among the colonists. It all started soon after the Littles arrived, was at its peak when they went back to India but the threat was receding by the time they returned. Or was it an opportunity being lost? It depended on which side of the debate you were on. The subject was American whalers.

The report in the local papers that only fourteen ocean going ships visited Swan River in 1838 was not completely true. This number excluded whaling ships of which there were many and most had sailed from America so were certainly ocean going. These were not considered part of the colony's business. They were seen as outsiders, a threat to trade and even to the political security of the colony. The fact that they taxed the minds of the colonists a great deal, perhaps gives an insight into the insecurity and fragility of the new colony.

The supposed threat from these ships and the fact that they regularly landed and set up temporary settlements was one of the factors that led to the proclamation of the west of Australia as a British colony. These men and their whaling ships had been visiting Australian waters since the 1790s and wintered in sheltered bays such as Swan River, Albany and Koombana Bay. But Britain had been at war with America as recently as 1812 – 1814 and, along with the Dutch and French, why should America not claim this new land. At their peak in 1840 – 1842 there were perhaps a hundred American whaling ships fishing off the coast and, no doubt, it is these ships which are shown in Louisa Clifton's watercolour on the front cover of this book. Their crews outnumbered colonial inhabitants and land-based settlements by whalers were firmly discouraged in case they became permanent and they took over. One such settlement was created after two whaling ships were wrecked in Koombana Bay in July 1840 and, naturally, the crews set up a temporary base on land. Some of them may have been on Thomas' land so he would have been very much involved. It was one of these buildings, and land, that Rev. Wollaston bought from Captain Coffin, a whaler, in 1841 which suggests that the whalers were indeed becoming established on land. Knowing Thomas and Eliza, they probably gave the whalers every assistance in their plight, despite some local opposition.

Many settlers also objected to the Americans fishing in the colony's waters, within three miles of the coast, thinking that they would so deplete whale stocks that it would prevent a home-grown whaling industry from developing. But local attempts at whaling failed as local men did not have the skills or equipment. The authorities did not like the way the American ships operated and traded outside the law, avoiding duty on items they sold. They acted as if they owned the place! Naturally the whalers came ashore looking for fresh water, fresh meat and other supplies and, as their numbers grew, trade did develop to the extent that many ships left their American home ports with supplies of all sorts from clothing and hardware to cheese and clocks which were welcome at smaller settlements such as Bunbury which only got second pickings of goods from Britain after they had passed through Fremantle and Perth. These items were traded for local produce and this was very welcome.

The influence of whalers dropped significantly after the mid 1840s. This was partly due to the number of whales having been reduced dramatically but also because the whalers were not welcome. High port and pilot fees were introduced at Fremantle and Albany and the whalers accused the local people of charging exorbitant prices for their goods. But the locals said the whalers took so much that it put all prices up, which, of course pleased the farmers. There were so many sides to this great debate. All this led the whalers to make more use of smaller anchorages such as Koombana Bay for a while and local farmers there benefitted from the increased demand for their vegetables and other goods. But the number of whalers shrank dramatically and many local people said that the opportunity of turning Western Australia into a major supply base for fleets in the Indian and Pacific Oceans had been lost.

WESTERN AUSTRALIA

CHAPTER 11

RISE

The preceding background is important to set the scene but, whatever its shortcomings, Western Australia was to be Thomas and Eliza's home for the rest of their lives. Thomas was to go down in history as a founding pioneer of Western Australia and Eliza played no small part in their success.

On his return in March 1843 Prinsep's business was developed in earnest by Thomas Little. He brought with him 30 horses, and many horses that Prinsep kept on his estate in Tasmania were gradually transferred to Western Australia so they could be nearer the market for them in India. From his initial purchase in 1839, to his final purchase of 20,000 acres (8100 hectares) in 1850, Thomas bought new and better land and built up an estate of 23,277 acres (9400 hectares) for Charles Prinsep.

It is the plan of Belvidere, their house and grounds, shown opposite, that gives an interesting insight into Thomas' and Eliza's lives in 1847 and it is worth spending a moment studying it. We shall hear a lot about winemaking later and the plan shows about 2 acres (¾ hectare) of vineyards with 3000 stakes so this was well established

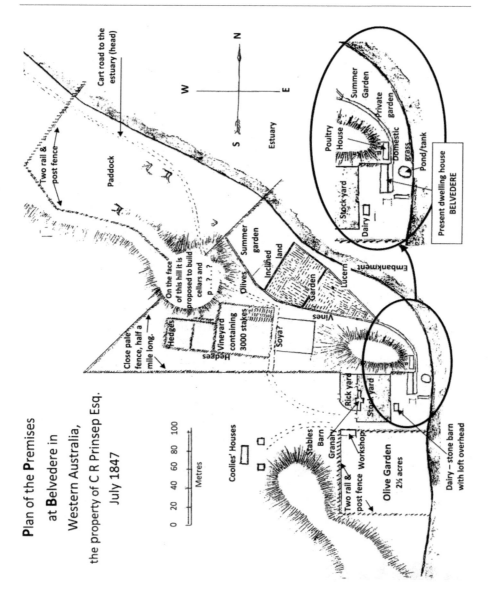

Plan of the Premises at Belvedere in Western Australia, the property of C R Prinsep Esq. July 1847

Cart road to the estuary (head)

Two rail & post fence

Paddock

Estuary

On the face of this hill it is proposed to build cellars and p . ? . ?

Hedges

Close pale fence, half a mile long.

Vineyard containing 3000 stakes

Hedges

Olives

Summer garden

Inclined land

Garden

Soya?

Lucern

Vines

Embankment

Summer Garden

Poultry House

Private garden

Domestic grass

Pond/tank

Stock yard

Dairy

Present dwelling house BELVEDERE

Metres

0 20 40 60 80 100

Coolies' Houses

Rick yard

Stock yard

Stables

Barn

Granary

Workshop

Two rail & post fence

Olive Garden 2½ acres

Dairy – stone barn with loft overhead

This plan of the Belvidere estate has been re-drawn for clarity as much of the writing in this old document had become difficult to read. The original was found in 'Excellent Connections – A History of Bunbury, Western Australia, 1836 – 1990' by Anthony J Barker and Maxine Laurie, published by the City of Bunbury.

by now. But there is also a 2½ acre (1 hectare) olive garden, big enough for commercial production, but we hear nothing of olives elsewhere. Were these ventures on behalf of Charles Prinsep or was this Thomas already branching out on his own? Soya and lucern were also being grown in sufficient quantity to be represented on the plan and this was probably for animal feed. Any good farm would have a dairy and poultry house. The triangular area marked 'Garden' was not what we would think of as a garden today. It was for vegetables and the plan is marked out in this way. Nearly everybody in England or Ireland who had a piece of land would put it to use to support the family with vegetables and it was even more important for Thomas and Eliza to do this as they couldn't just go to market to buy them. Flower gardens were only for the wealthy who had space and time for such a luxury and these were known as 'Pleasure Gardens' to differentiate them from a vegetable plot. So what were the 'Private Garden' and the 'Summer Garden', as shown on the plan? It suggests a Pleasure Garden for their own relaxation; laid out with lawn and flowers. They cover two large areas on the plan so does this suggest that Thomas and Eliza had the spare time, or servants, and money to indulge in this? Was this Eliza' influence? Nothing elsewhere suggests that Thomas was other than a man of constant activity.

As early as 1845 there was a Vineyard Society in Western Australia and Thomas is mentioned in the report of its annual meeting in April of that year when one of the debates was how to rid vineyards of the scourge of birds. 'Silvereyes' arrive in their hundreds just as the grapes ripen and decimate the crop just before the harvest. Thomas reported great success with tame hawks which frighten the birds away. The following year he joined by post in a debate on infestations of caterpillars. He reported that they only attacked his Verdeihlo, Muscatel and Frontignac vines which had been imported from The Cape of Good Hope so he believes the creatures came in on the imported young vines. The Society report praised Thomas for his studies of these subjects and in each case reporting a cure. This was his cure for caterpillars.

> "He (Thomas) adds, moreover, the gratifying intelligence that he thinks he has succeeded in extirpating the whole race in his locality by preventing the formation of a single chrysalis in his vineyard. This has been done by going over the vines three times a day with a number of hands and is proof of the unwearied perseverance of this very zealous member of the Society."

At the end of 1846 Thomas presented the members with trays of his figs which were deemed to be as good as any from Turkey. This typifies his willingness to experiment with new crops and his attention to detail in analysing reasons for success or failure. In May 1850 it was reported in the press that Thomas sent a sample of his figs to Prinsep in Calcutta. Overleaf, on page 140, is the frontispiece of a book owned by Thomas; '*Loudon's Encyclopedia of Gardening'*, printed in 1824. It has hundreds of pages describing techniques, varieties of plants and how they fare in different climates. This is a book for a man of detail.

Thomas and all the other settlers also had to contend with extremes of weather in establishing their crops and livelihoods. As well as poor soil in places, the weather was frequently too hot and dry in the summer and too wet in winter. In July 1849 the area was flooded after heavy rains and the Littles' kitchen gardens and flower gardens were submerged for several days. The land of the Wollastons, Ommannys, Cliftons and Scotts was severely damaged and the house of a Mr Gregory was washed away. Nevertheless, Belvidere was ready for a visit by the Governor in December 1850. He was touring the area in a brand-new, four-wheel carriage drawn by two horses and he had lunch with Thomas and Eliza before spending the afternoon inspecting the "stud of horses and fine gardens, etc."

The growth of the Colony as a whole remained slow and press reports suggest the settlers were desperate to find goods they could export at a profit. As we have seen, whaling had been the big thing at one time but got nowhere partly because of local infighting. Timber seemed to be the only natural resource of any value and in 1847 and 1848 the local press was full of this opportunity. In 1847, after a public meeting, there was a united effort to journey into the hinterland to start felling timber for export. This was the first joint enterprise among settlers, often known for their competitiveness rather than cooperation, but success and profit were proving hard to find and the potential of this timber project was seen as being big enough to overcome old rivalries. Two of the Clifton sons were to be expedition leaders and Thomas Little was to provide wagons and bullocks. In January 1848 a ship, *Salween*, called into Bunbury because it had been greatly delayed on its voyage from India and was in desperate need of fresh water. Before sailing on to Hobart with its 7 passengers, 29 prisoners, 15 soldiers and 36 crew, the captain agreed to return with horses for Thomas Little and to pick up

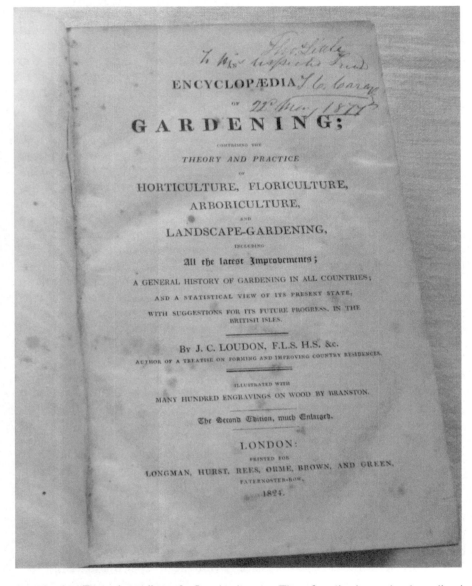

Loudon's Encyclopedia of Gardening. The frontispiece is inscribed "Thomas Little, to his respected friend, J C Carey. 22nd May 1877". It is dated just a few weeks before Thomas' death.

a full load of 9 foot jarrah wood railway sleepers for India. The captain said he could take eight or nine ship loads a year. This news fuelled the optimism but also demonstrates how Thomas, and other settlers, did business. They grasped opportunities; a stray ship and a deal done. Unfortunately, the timber trade, like other hopes, did well for a few years but then fell way below the level of the original expectations.

A few years later, on 2nd March 1853, great excitement was caused in the Bunbury area by the arrival of the first steam ship in their port. *HMS Torch* was an iron paddle-wheel steam vessel of 350 tons and her arrival was a big enough event to be recorded in the Bunbury column of the Perth Gazette. The story throws light on the lives of the local people and also on the travails of this new technology. *Torch* called at Bunbury in the hope of taking on firewood which had not been available at Fremantle. There was a store of firewood at Bunbury in readiness for the winter and it was decided to sell this for *Torch* and replace it after she had gone. Soon eight or ten teams

HMS Herald on the left with HMS Torch behind, sketched as they were leaving England.　　　　*Illustrated London News, 15th May 1852*

were carting the wood down to the beach. It took two days to load the wood using *Torch's* own boats and a 'flat' lent by Thomas Little. The flat was a flat bottomed, wide, rectangular barge which Thomas used for transporting goods and livestock across the estuary.

Torch's officers were entertained by the local gentlemen and taken to see the neighbourhood, including a shaft being dug in the hope of mining coal. No doubt, over dinners, the fascinating stories of *Torch's* purpose and the problems of the latest technology would have been discussed in detail.

Torch was the tender ship to *HMS Herald* (500 tons), both of which had left London on 10th June 1852. Their purpose was to survey the Australian coast and Fiji Islands and on board the Herald were botanists and zoologists as well as surveyors. *Torch's* purpose was to sail into narrow or shallow inlets, act as supply ship to the Herald and even tow *Herald* if need be. *Herald* had eight guns and *Torch* one gun. Soon after leaving London it was found that *Torch* could not raise her paddles out of the water when under sail, as she was designed to do, and the resulting drag considerably reduced her speed under sail. Hence the urgent need for firewood. Unable to get repairs in Madeira the two ships carried on but lost contact in the Indian Ocean. *Torch* eventually arrived in Sydney on 7th April, the journey from London having taken ten months and the ship having been written off by many as lost at sea as no word had been received of her safety.

Torch towed Thomas' flat back up the estuary to Belvidere and sailed at sunrise on the fourth day after her arrival, just as *Rosebud* unexpectedly arrived. A deal was struck with *Rosebud's* captain that he should return empty from 'The Swan' and take on a cargo of timber for the Eastern Colonies. He brought news of the success of many in the goldfields. Meanwhile two mail ships from the east had failed to arrive as expected. Such was the way of life, the slow motion and erratic travel by sea, the way of trade and the keen interest in any news from outside.

The breeding of horses was Thomas' original aim. They were a high value product but their transport was risky. In bad weather they had to be hung by slings under their chest and stomach in a ship to prevent them falling or panicking and injuring themselves. It was normal for a ship's captain to demand payment for his shipping services before any cargo was unloaded but on one occasion, in

March 1850, Thomas was persuaded to pay before he was even allowed on board. Having paid, what he found was that only four out of twenty of his horses arriving from Tasmania were alive. This disaster was caused by bad seas and disease which took hold in their cramped quarters below deck. In the same year a man died from a kick from a horse on board a ship.

21st October 1851 saw the marriage of Thomas and Eliza's adopted daughter, Maria Glynn, to Charley Clifton, one of the sons of Waller Clifton, a great family friend and, as we have seen, one of the large landowners in the area. The day was recorded in Waller Clifton's diary. The marriage rites of the Catholic church were not recognised by the State, hence the second ceremony which they shared with Charley's sister Rachel.

21st October 1851: 'A most brilliant Day. Lucy, Charles and I embarked at 7 in the whale boat and went to Belvidere. Charley & Maria were there married according to the forms of the Roman Catholic Church by the Rev. Mr Donovan R.C. After breakfast we four preceded in the whale boat to Australind. After collecting the whole party, we preceded to

HMS Torch after she eventually reached Sidney. Painted in 1855 by Conrad Martens. State Library of NSW

the Old Church where Rachel & George Smith and Charley & Maria Glynn were married in one service. The Littles and John Bussell, Bedingfelds and Bunbury arrived to the breakfast and the whole of our family and all the children sat down to it. George Smith and his wife retired to Locks and Charley & Maria went to Bury Hill. The party remained. We had dancing till 2 o'clock and all slept here from the Boisterous Night.'

This was Waller Clifton's view but the joy of the occasion was not to last and was to be the cause of the Littles falling out with Maria; losing her, in fact. Maria married into the influential family headed by Waller Clifton who became increasingly anti Catholic, to the extent that it is a wonder the marriage was ever allowed. Waller was on the Legislative Assembly of Western Australia and he is on record denouncing Catholic activities. In 1853 four ship loads of Irish Catholic girls arrived from Dublin and Cork – 400 girls in total. These became known as bride ships because, as well as providing much needed domestic labour, the girls were to be wives to the unruly single working class men and convicts. There was considered to be no better way of curbing the irregular habits of these men than their union with a discreet, frugal, industrious female immigrant who would turn their husband's mind to caring for their family. Waller Clifton objected to "*the stamp of these immigrant girls and especially the infusion of Catholic girls*". He was afraid they might spread their faith through their children. Yet just two years earlier Waller's own son had married a Catholic girl, Maria.

Married.

At Australind, on the 21st Inst., by the Rev. Mathew Fletcher, A.M., GEORGE SMITH, Esq., second son of Charles Henry Smith, Esq., late Storekeeper of Malta Dockyard, to RACHEL CATHARINE, fifth daughter of M. Waller Clifton, Esq., F.R.S., M.C.

At the same place and time, also by the Rev. Mathew Fletcher, (the ceremony having been previously solemnized at Belvedere, according to the forms of the Roman Catholic Church, by the Rev. T. Donovan, R.C.C.,) CHARLES HIPPUFF CLIFTON, ESq., seventh surviving son of M. Waller Clifton, Esq., to MARIA GLYNN, the adopted daughter of Thomas Little, Esq., J.P., of Belvedere.

The announcement of the marriage of Maria Glynn as reported in the Perth Gazette on 31st October 1851

It seems that Maria had insisted, according to Catholic custom, that Charley Clifton convert to Catholicism and any children should be raised as Catholics. Rev. Wollaston, in his journal tells of a visit to the Littles the March prior to the marriage when Maria was there.

> *"Maria, I suppose, will be married soon – Charles has turned nominally R. Catholic (not 'turned' – but become – he was nothing before.)"*

With Waller Clifton as a father-in-law it is not surprising that this arrangement did not last. Rev. Wollaston's note after he visited again in March 1853 infers that the reason for the split was to do with religion.

> *"Grieved to find an irreconcilable schism had arisen between this family (the Littles) and the Cliftons, caused by the marriage of Mr Little's ward with one of Mr Clifton's sons. There are faults on both sides but poor Mr and Mrs Little are completely governed by their priest and become sadly bigoted."*

Maria seems to have renounced her faith, the faith that was so important to Thomas and Eliza and which they may have promised her dying parents to preserve. They had loved Maria as their own child and this must have been extremely hard to bear. The Littles and Cliftons fell out over this and Waller's intolerance of Catholics in general. But Waller Clifton was a strongly opinionated man, his aggression probably exacerbated by his realisation by now that the dream of Australind would fail. He even fell out with the Anglican priest who was another of his sons-in-law, to the extent that the son-in-law moved to Busselton taking his wife, Waller's daughter, with him.

The other couple in that joint marriage fared even worse. Rachel (née Clifton) died in childbirth the following July. Her husband, George, died three weeks later and the baby died in September, all within a year of this joyous marriage. Life was hard.

It was normal in India for an officer or employee to develop a business or businesses of his own and Thomas continued this tradition in Australia. He had been buying land on his own account and in 1852 he acquired the largest holding of his own, 12,300 acres at one auction. Although he didn't buy this land but leased it for eight years, this shows his confidence in being able to run a profitable business of his own. With local timber and bricks made on the site he began building a grand mansion there, which he named Dardanup Park. It was completed in three stages by 1858 and this timetable can only have been due to financial constraints. What a difference it was to the humble beginning in life that both Thomas and Eliza had had in Ireland. It was a beautiful two storey house with a large banqueting room fit for the large dinner parties that the Littles were renowned for. There were three more large living rooms, all with high ceilings, large windows and impressive fireplaces. Completing the whole, when the three phases were finished, was a grand entrance hall from which rose a magnificent sweeping staircase, 22 steps high to a gallery and five bedrooms. It boasted the ultimate luxury, a separate indoor bathroom. This was a rock solid house with walls two feet thick with the distinctive brickwork pattern of Flemish Bond.

The original old farmhouse was retained behind the new house, perhaps to accommodate the servants and where there was the laundry and schoolroom. In order to house his collection of fine wines and in view of his plans for his wine business, below the main house were four large cellars. However, these are said to have been used as dormitories for his Chinese workers who tended the vines. The house is still there today, extended slightly and it is still the most impressive mansion in the area, described as a masterpiece of craftsmanship in recent sales literature.

In 1854, Thomas left the employment of Charles Prinsep. He had held the post for sixteen years which was a very long time for a manager to be in position so Prinsep must have been happy with or indifferent to his work. Sources differ as to why he left. Rev. Wollaston claimed that for years after he left, Thomas was aggrieved at being asked to leave. Others say that with the returns never matching Prinsep's aspirations, the obvious person to blame was the manager – Thomas Little – and a new manager was installed who was no more successful. However, Charles Prinsep had a major stroke in India the following year and retired to London to live out his life as an invalid and his son recorded how loyal to his father Thomas had been. Did Charles Prinsep know that Thomas was accumulating and managing his own land at the same time as being employed by him, building up an estate of his own? He probably assumed he was as this was what would have happened in India. Whatever the reason, you cannot serve two masters and run two businesses at the same time. Thomas was 54 and Eliza was 57 and they must have thought it was now or never for any dream they might have had of breaking out on their own.

Now on his own, Thomas was to develop a major farming enterprise that brought him a good income for ten years, from his own land and from tenant farmers. He concentrated on cattle and grain, particularly corn, and also had large orchards, olive groves and vineyards. He became a major wine producer and this is said to have been his main source of income.

We have seen earlier that Thomas was growing vines at Belvidere and now he produced sweet red wines and fine red Constantia, a grape from South Africa. There are numerous reports in the newspapers of his wine winning prizes at local agricultural shows and in a June 1866 report on the state of the Colony he was mentioned as a major wine producer. That report added that the largest vineyards were only ten acres yet it is reported elsewhere that Thomas had 45,000 vines at the peak. Modern grape planting for wine varies between 1000 vines per acre (2m x 2m spacing) and 4000 vines per acre (1m x 1m spacing) so 45,000 vines on ten acres would seem to be very crowded. However, the numbers and acreage would have been approximations and these reports certainly confirm that he was a major producer.

At its peak he produced 12,000 bottles a year which means that he must have exported most of his wine. Much wine was exported to other Australian colonies but surviving reports of Thomas' attempts to export around the world are those of his failures rather than his successes. In 1859 he sent a consignment to London on the *Dolphin*. The captain put it in his cabin for safe keeping but the bottles all arrived in London empty. The captain had drunk it all. In 1860 he sent a consignment to Colombo, Ceylon but when it arrived the wine had lost all strength and sweetness but, mysteriously, had not turned sour. Only the colour remained. Thomas' conclusion was that the bottles had been tampered with and the wine replaced with coloured water.

The remembrances of the Sisters of Mercy and of J T Reilly are the earliest and nearest to an original source and both confirm that Thomas was a major wine producer. Both say that he won prizes in shows both locally and at the Sydney World Fair of 1863. But his greatest success must have been at the International Exhibition in

London in 1862. The Great Exhibition of 1851 had been copied in many parts of the world, but never equalled. The repeat in 1862 was meant to be its equal and certainly came close. It had 28,000 catalogued exhibits with many late entries taking it to 30,000 at least. Exhibitors came from every corner of the globe; from Russia to the USA, the many nation states of Europe and all the British colonies from Newfoundland to Australia and tiny islands from Hayti to Mayotte & Nossi-Be. There were seventy Classes of products for every conceivable manufactured, farmed or quarried product and the catalogue clearly showed the dominance and pulling power of London as the capital of the world.

The first mention of the Exhibition in the Western Australian press was in February 1861, only fourteen months before the opening, with complaints that the colony's plans were running late. Individuals could not enter as states were required to set up Central Committees. Other Australian colonies were up and running. It was not until May 1861 that the Governor set up a Central Committee in Perth and a warehouse for selecting display items in the Mechanics Institute. By the end of May, local sub-committees were set up and the Bunbury and Australind Committee consisted of W Pearce Clifton (one of Waller Clifton's sons), George Elliott (Louisa Clifton's husband) and Thomas Little. This was one of six local committees to cover areas outside the central area of Perth and Fremantle.

From then on there were reports in all the newspapers as enthusiasm increased. It was one of the matters that involved everybody and Thomas was, as usual, in the thick of it. It must be remembered that the European population of the vast area of Western Australia in 1861 was still only 15,593, as shown in the 1861 census. Everybody knew or had heard of everybody else and projects such as this brought people together in a common cause with much to talk about and compare.

The purpose of sub-committees, like Thomas', was to select the best items from each class, locally, for submission to the Central Committee who would select, again, the best from the whole colony. This clearly had the likelihood of being contentious and, in the end, about 85 items were selected from about 60 people. All three men on Thomas' committee had items selected and there did seem to be a preponderance of items from members of the committees. Western Australian entries ranged from ores, timbers and furs, to furniture, wheat, wool, wine, olive oil and culinary seaweed, to pressed flowers and a muff of parrot feathers from the Misses Lukin and Knight. There is no list of items rejected but one offering lauded in the press but not selected was seven stuffed alpacas, aimed at demonstrating the quality of their fleece.

The items for exhibition were shipped on *Gloucester* which was due to sail in December but did not leave till 7th January 1862, just 15 weeks before the exhibition opened. On board was the retiring Governor and his family. The ship was delayed at Cape Town and arrived in London docks just seven days before the opening and the agent managed to get the goods to the site with just two days to go. Here he was confronted with a jam of wagons, with carters sleeping under them so as not to lose their place in the queue. The agent had had to furnish his space without knowing what items he had to display so borrowed relevant objects from friends in London. So the largest item on display was a huge glass case containing two stuffed black swans with five cygnets.

Naturally he complained bitterly about this and also his lack of information, particularly on the prices of products, and this generated recriminations back in Western Australia. He said that the number of items and quality was very poor compared with other Australian colonies which put on magnificent decorative displays which he did not have the budget for. Tasmania featured a polished wooden tower with a staircase inside and viewing platform on top. New South Wales had a case of nuggets of gold. He said that he had to be on duty at all hours, without an assistant, and employ guards from his own money to prevent theft.

This generated great debate which was recorded in the Perth newspapers. Interestingly for our story of Thomas and his small community, the debate moved from throwing accusations at the Governor for parsimony, at the colonists for apathy and the Central and Local Committees for leaving things so late, to a more reasoned realisation of the state of the colony. New South Wales, which had such a grand display, had a population of 351,000, twenty two times the size of Western Australia and many more times its wealth, so they could afford to send more products and put on a better display. Victoria, with a population of 514,000, thirty three times the size, was ejected from the Exhibition for failing to take up their space by the deadline and, only after much negotiation, was able to erect their stand at night and open its display a week after the show had opened.

All argument was put aside when the list of winners of medals arrived. The big prize was an enormous bronze medal (shown actual size, opposite) and Western Australia won fourteen of them, Thomas Little being one of the winners. It also won twelve Honourable Mentions. Six of Western Australia's entries were wine and Thomas' wine was the only one to win a medal. It was for "the General Excellence of his Wines", from a Black Frontignac grape grown in a soil of decomposed granite. None of the others even won an Honourable Mention. For Thomas to win such an award on the world stage was a significant achievement and must have been the cause of great rejoicing in the Little household.

A total of 6992 medals were awarded, which was fewer than a quarter of the exhibitors. At that rate, with 85 entries, Western Australia may have earned eighteen or nineteen. But Western Australia was a new and tiny colony with little industry, undercapitalised and with other skills in their infancy, and it was competing against the greatest, inventors, industrialists, farmers and artists in the world. So fourteen medals was considered an exceptional performance. Press articles talked of a pride in sending products "home" to such acclaim. The prestige attached to winning such an award can be demonstrated by the fact that one of Britain's first pieces of consumer protection legislation (The Exhibition Medals Act 1863) made it a criminal offence to state or imply that you had won a medal when you had not.

The exhibition hall in London dwarfed most buildings in the world. Average daily attendance over the six months, at 37,600, was two and a half times the entire British population of Western Australia. Yet the little guy won!

For Thomas to have achieved this success must have been hard work and it showed his dedication to perfection, not only in the growing of grapes but in the fermentation, bottling, other processes and sales. It was a tragedy that, as we shall see later, events had already conspired to prevent him capitalising on this success.

The magnificent medal presented to Thomas and other winners is shown actual size. It was heavy bronze, 3" (77mm) in diameter and had a satin lined case. It was inscribed round the rim   THOMAS LITTLE -   CLASS III Where is it now?

One of Thomas' many other talents and passions was horses. Although he doesn't seem to have bred them commercially any more, he was a judge at horse shows, a race steward and on the committee of the Bunbury Horse Racing Club. Horse racing had been carried out in Western Australia from the early days but the first race in Bunbury was in January 1854 and horses trained by Thomas won three of the six races. In 1856 two of the four races were won by horses ridden by Thomas Jr. At that meeting there was a pony race, perhaps for children, and a hack stakes won by William Little against thirteen runners. In 1857, at Bunbury, a horse that Thomas trained, Bussell, won both its races, carrying off a £22 prize for each. Thomas Sr. and Thomas Jr. were also very active in training, riding and stewarding at Bunbury.

This enthusiasm was carried further by Thomas Jr. who was reported in January 1865 to be living in Melbourne as a professional horse trainer. A first class horse of his, named Ben Bolt, was taken to Hobart to take part in the Great Champion Stakes in November 1861. Twenty two top horses from all over Australia were to take part for an enormous prize of 2,000 guineas and the eyes of all Western Australia were on it. But the day before the race Ben Bolt was injured. Thomas' request for the race to be delayed for a day was refused and Ben Bolt ran lame but still came fifth. Thomas Jr. sold Ben Bolt there for £160, which seems a very small amount for such a horse that had the ability to win such prestigious and lucrative races. He later regretted this as Ben Bolt became a very successful and famous horse, winning many valuable races. Thomas Sr. wrote to his friend Fr. Garrido about the Great Champion Stakes and the letter shows his religious attitude, his fondness of his son and the ever present fear that a long sea voyage may bring disaster. He also refers to "we" so seems to be writing on behalf of Eliza too.

> . . . . . I suppose you have heard of Thomas' adventure in Tasmania and of his disappointment. He would have enjoyed the trip very much but for the accident to the horse which, humanly speaking, deprived him of some 3 to 4 thousand pounds. We were not so much disappointed as he was for we were not so sanguine of his success; still so far as the ability of the horse and trainer were concerned he could not have but won. However, it was clearly the will of God, for good and wise purposes, that he should not win and

that is all we need to say but to bless His Holy Will who brought him back safe to us.

It was reported in the Perth Gazette in March 1866 that another horse bred by Thomas, Star of the South, was sold to a Mr Brown of Madras where it easily won the prestigious Rajah of Vigianagnam's plate.

Thomas Sr. was also fond of going off into the country on horseback with his friends, hunting, exploring and getting away from it all. Not only was it a pleasant holiday but he would also have been on the lookout for new land and business opportunities. On more than one occasion he went with a crowd of Australind settlers to help them find new land as holdings needed to be bigger than they already had, in order to be viable.

Thomas was involved in all aspects of the community. As early as 1842 he was a member of the Town Trust, the local council, even before it was legally constituted. By 1851 he was a Justice of the

Another sketch from the Illustrated London News of 14th March 1857 shows a kangaroo hunt at Culham. A kangaroo hunt provided great sport and also reasonable meat and the hope that these pests would be exterminated – a fanciful desire and one which shows a different way of thinking in those days.

Peace (JP) and he is reported as presiding at a murder trial in December 1855. He maintained this role for the rest of his life. Also in 1852 he was on the committee raising funds for a Catholic church in Fremantle. In 1862 he was elected to the committee of the Southern District Agricultural Society, set up that year with the aim of organising the first agricultural show. He was a man who could not sit still but enjoyed volunteering and being at the heart of everything the community was doing.

The diaries kept by the Littles' neighbours describe the social life of the area, in which the Littles were very much involved. The absence of wider family was made up for by neighbours who frequently met and stayed with each other, perhaps for days, because of the distance to travel or if the weather turned bad or if the party went on too late. Often children were left behind with friends of their own age. Mary Wollaston, being of a very nervous disposition, hardly ever travelled. Rev. Wollaston was often away for periods carrying out his church duties and she would frequently go and stay with Eliza Little who would send a boat across the estuary to collect her and her girls. Mary was a very fastidious lady, abhorring dirt and untidiness. She and her husband were often appalled by the dirt, insect infestations and untidiness they encountered when visiting the homes of settlers so the fact that she felt most happy at Belvidere tells us something about Eliza's housekeeping.

Often, because of the difficulty of communication, guests would arrive unannounced. Such a situation saw the introduction of the first Catholic priest, just arrived in the colony. Back in January 1844 a John Gibson met him, the Rev. Dr. Brady, on the road and stopped to talk, as one always did. Dr. Brady asked the way to Mr Little's house and John Gibson knew because he was to be the new teacher for the Little boys, Thomas Jr. and William. Gibson was a graduate of Cambridge University so probably an excellent choice as a tutor. He was on the way to the Wollastons and this encounter was reported to Rev. Wollaston who was dismayed by the arrival of a papist priest, and Irish too. Poor Rev. Wollaston was torn between his fear, almost hatred, of Catholics and the threat they posed and his great friendship with the Littles. Thomas and Wollaston were able to debate religious matters, fiercely at times, but each always failed to convert the other. It was a back-handed compliment from the Rev. Wollaston when he said of the Littles in August 1844;

"The Littles are such excellent, benevolent people that I regret every time I see them, more and more, that they are Papists."

Despite all this, the Rev. Dr. Brady received a very warm welcome when he arrived at Belvidere. The Littles were honoured and delighted by the unexpected arrival of a person who had travelled especially to see them and he was obviously invited to stay. The following day Thomas took Rev. Brady to meet the Cliftons who invited them back to lunch the following day where they had a pleasant few hours together; all recorded in Louisa's diary. Rev. Brady was a scholar with a doctorate from the University of Paris so brought interesting news from abroad which was always welcome. Louisa was impressed by his plans to help the poor Irish and educate their children and to bring the aborigines into the fold. Thomas quickly passed an invitation to Mass to local Catholics and this was performed in Belvidere on the Sunday morning. It was a wonderful weekend for Thomas and Eliza. Several baptisms were carried out at Belvidere during Rev Brady's stay.

A similar situation occurred eight years later and it is included in our story as it demonstrates the importance of the Littles to the Catholic Church and gives an insight into modes of travel and timescales at that time. Thomas' importance can be judged by the fact that in 1851 he was joint Chairman of the committee formed to raise funds for a new Catholic church in Fremantle, 90 miles from his home and presumably involving several day-long boat trips up and down the coast. From about this time the infant Catholic Church in Western Australia was being wracked by arguments between two priests who both claimed the title of Bishop of Western Australia; Rev. Serra and Rev. Brady. Thomas was heavily involved in this as representative of his region on the group in favour of Rev. Serra. His group garnered 305 votes for Rev Serra from local Catholics while the opposing group could only muster about 200 but this was not a clear enough majority to settle the issue.

The Archbishop of all Australia, John Polding, set out from Sydney by ship to resolve the issue. He landed at Albany on the south coast to dedicate a new Catholic church there but then declined to continue his journey by sea, supposedly because the weather was so bad that he feared the sea journey round the south west cape. It is also likely that he wanted to meet Thomas Little before he arrived in Perth. So he,

. . . . . bought a good horse and with a great storm coming on and escorted by a policeman to show him the way, he headed towards Kojonup and disappeared into the timber.

A week later, after a 210 mile journey he arrived at Belvidere, very tired and bedraggled on 12th June 1852. (Remember, this is in the middle of the Australian winter) Either Thomas Jr or William was sent urgently by horse, as there were no ships, through the storm to Perth to make a dramatic intervention in a civil court case taking place between the two rivals. This intervention was a summons from the Archbishop that Rev. Brady should appear before him at Belvidere. Rev. Brady set out but changed his mind and retreated to Perth. The Archbishop stayed with the Littles for several weeks before travelling to Perth to finally bring the dispute to an end in favour of the new Bishop Serra.

At the same time, dated 15th June, Thomas sent two letters to the newspapers stating that anybody spending money on behalf of the Catholic Church would be held personally liable for losses unless that expenditure was authorised by the Bishop, Rev John Bede Polding. He signed these letters as "Acting Secretary to His Grace, The Archbishop Metropolitan" who was staying with him at Belvidere.

So far, stories of all this activity have only involved Thomas. However, Eliza also led a busy life that would have revolved around running the house and managing the home farm, probably with a few cows to be milked in a dairy and maybe some pigs. There had to be vegetable gardens as they would have needed to be self sufficient. This may well have been a skill Eliza learnt from her father but she would have had help. In the early days it was the job of the wives of the Indian hill coolies to help her in the house and kitchen gardens and later she would have had other servants, perhaps the wives of tenants. There was cooking, baking and preserving to be done – bottling fruit and vegetables and salting meat and fish. She also kept turkeys as these are often mentioned in Louisa Clifton's and Rev. Wollaston's diaries. With a population under a hundred there were no shops as we would know them in Bunbury so barter was a common means of trade. Eliza often exchanged turkeys, in one case for some fabrics just arrived from England. At another time Mary Wollaston did not have enough grain for her two turkeys so Eliza took them to add to her flock, to be returned later. She gave Mrs Wollaston a silk bonnet.

Adverts such as this were placed by traders after the arrival of a ship from England. They described all the goods he had ordered and which were now available. This advert appeared in January 1856 and shows consignments received on the ships 'Swan' and 'Avalanche'

Arrival of goods from England or India was always a cause of excitement. There were dealers in agricultural equipment and some other goods were manufactured locally. There were general dealers and a wine merchant in Perth but there was always something that had to be ordered. The local newspapers carried advertisements from English manufacturers but by the time a letter had been sent, payment arranged and delivery made from England, six months or a year could pass. For Eliza and her many lady friends the arrival of fabrics, clothing and news of the latest fashions was anticipated and discussed at length. And these ships carried mail to and from family and friends at home and it is known that, at least, Eliza's family knew of her doings.

Eliza would also have been in charge of entertaining which was a function she was renowned for. Just as they frequently stayed with friends, so friends stayed with them. The Littles had a reputation for never turning anyone away, whether he be an Irishman, a friend or a complete stranger passing through the area. Their door was always open and their parties were often mixed and lively as the following description shows. The following report is taken from George Russo's book in which he quotes, in italics, from Louisa Clifton's diary. It is a wonderful description of Thomas and Eliza and the society they inhabited. Louisa was about 26 and had been in Swan River only a few weeks. It could easily have been taken straight from a Jane Austen novel.

Little was an excellent host and his home became a centre of Irish hospitality. On one occasion a party arrived to sample some of that hospitality; one a captain of a trading vessel, "two colonials", a sheep drover who had brought sheep to Bunbury for sale and some members of the Australind settlers, including Waller, Elinor and Louisa Clifton, who were intent on "observing colonial society".

"How little captivating or refined it is! Captain Symes is a rough but rather pleasing man; Mr. Jepson, (who captained the Gaillardon that brought the Littles to Swan River) vulgar and unprepossessing, young, rough and, of course, in dress, to English eyes, anything but a gentleman. The want of gentlemanly dress is an additional friction to taste."

Louisa wanted to see some culture, some real refinement but how was it to be achieved in this wilderness? She was fast changing her mind about civilisation being among the settlers. It was hardly known.

As Louisa was thinking along these lines the young men decided to act "naturally". Captain Coffin (the captain of a whaling ship whose ramshackle house the Wollastons had just bought) had arrived to boost their confidence and they were roused to bid him welcome in the form of a "farewell" as he was poised to leave for Nantucket, his home in America.

Little, accustomed to entertaining visiting travellers, opened his wine cellar and invited all to stay for dinner. By the time the ladies had arrived many of the young men were feeling quite merry. Dr. Carpenter was in his element, feeling "at home" in his host's house.

The men continued their merriment into the night, one calling for an Irish ditty, and Mrs Little rose to oblige. She seemed to fit in with the visiting party. Elinor and Louisa both objected but said nothing. There was an obvious division among the guests; the male colonials and the cultured ladies, represented by Elinor and Louisa Clifton, with their Irish hosts comfortable with both sides. Louisa described it later as "a very stupid dinner".

On 1st June 1842 Louisa Clifton married George Elliott, the Resident Magistrate; a government employee, part of whose duties would be to act as magistrate and settle disputes, despite having no, or little, training in the law. Many local tradesmen were invited to the lavish wedding breakfast where they were served fresh meat, vegetables, plum pudding with plenty of London porter and a cask of wine. Entertainments throughout the afternoon included three hours of horse and foot races. Local aborigines entertained the guests in a spear throwing competition, winning loaves of bread and money that had been collected for them by the guests. In the evening a more select party sat down to a formal dinner. Thomas and Eliza would certainly have been at the afternoon festivities and probably also been invited to the dinner. The Cliftons seemed to have recreated an event that they had experienced at many an English country estate with everybody in their place, natives, tradesmen and the elite, but the Littles represented the typical settler who was much less bothered by such distinctions.

In 1860 William Little, their younger son, married Helena Mary Burke, an Irish girl, and the festivities are sure to have matched the occasion. She was a nurse who had come to Swan River via Plymouth on the 'bride ship', *Emma Eugenia* in May 1858. William and Helena had five children between 1861 and 1868. A boy and a girl died in infancy, leaving two girls and one boy. William, like all the family, was very active in horse racing in the 1850s being, at different times, Honorary Secretary and Clerk of the Course at Bunbury races and entering his own horse. He was also a keen cricketer, often playing with his brother in local matches.

The arrival of *Emma Eugenia* is ringed among the announcements opposite. A great argument erupted when she arrived because she brought 117 young single girls, nearly all from Ireland, and whose presumed bad character, loose morals, lack of patriotism and Romanist tendencies were expected to cause a lot of trouble. Despite the ship's captain reporting that only twelve of their number were "depraved" they proved, according to newspaper reports over the next year or so to be a valuable addition to the Colony. In fact it was said that the Irish girls were more hardworking, more grateful for the opportunities presented to them and settled down better than the English girls because the Irish girls were more used to hardship and the hard work expected in establishing the Colony. The arrival of the *Emma Eugenia* girls was not the first time that strong discrimination against Irish and Catholics had been highlighted. And Thomas and Eliza's son married one of the girls.

As has already been mentioned, this strong discrimination was a key aspect of Thomas and Eliza's lives because they were Catholics – and Irish too. This has been seen in their relationship with Rev. Wollaston but elsewhere such discrimination was far from as polite or reasoned as it was with Rev. Wollaston. Thomas and Eliza seem to have been very tolerant people, perhaps because Thomas' father was a Protestant, leading to them seeing both sides of the argument. Waller Clifton fell out with the Littles over religious differences but, generally, they managed to rise above the most bitter antagonism. However, openly promoting their Catholic faith and helping less fortunate Irish were the two strands that drove their

THE

I DEPENDENT JOURNAL,

Vox Populi, vox Dei.

FRIDAY, APRIL 30, 1858.

THE Mail from the Eastern Colonies arrived late last evening. By a hasty glance at our files, we have not been able to find much local intelligence of importance. South Australian papers of the 10th instant, quote Flour at £15 10s with a slight prospect of decline. Account sales of that forwarded to India are said to be very unfavourable.

At Melbourne business was very dull; the labor market is overdone, and the Government had determined to provide work for the unemployed at 4s per day. Coal sufficient to supply Melbourne for many years to come has been found at Cape Patterson, 15 miles from the coast.

The Sydney papers contain a month's later Calcutta news, received by H. M. S. "Megæra," arrived there to convey the 77th Regt. and a company of Artillery to India. The following are the most notable items :—

The Govenor-General had proceeded to the interior.

H.M.S. Himalaya had broken down and been sent to England with invalids and ladies and children, refugees from Lucknow, as a sailing vessel

Disturbances had occurred in Burmah, and Captain B. Seymour, H.M.S. Pelorus, had been despatched there with a naval brigade of 200 men.

The King of Delhi was on his trial. The proceedings had lasted five days, and were not terminated at the date advices left.

The system of flying coloumns was working extremely well. Several strong bodies of insurgents had been cut up or dispersed.

The troops of Jung Bahadoor, the Nepaulese Maharajah, had gained a great victory over the Rajah of Gondah.

THE Overland Mail of February 16th, arrived in Perth on Friday last about half-past twelve o'clock. The cause of its being so long behind time, was that the steamer *Columbian* had been out of coal for several days previous to arriving at the been off the harbour unable to get in from contrary winds. We have not much intelligence relating to this colony ; the despatches received by the Government contain no reference to the proposed alteration in the disposal of Crown Lands, or we believe to any other topic of general interest.

The *Indian Chief* sailed from the Downs on the 26th January, we have no list of passengers, but the *Home News* gives a list of the articles comprising her cargo, and there is scarcely an importer who has not had many of his packages shut out, owing to the large quantity of bottled beer she has on board.

The *Emma Eugenia*, M'Clelland, master, sailed from Plymouth on 10th Feb., with 187 Emigrants, consisting of 22 married couples, 5 single men, 117 single women, and 20 children, of whom 87 are English and 100 Irish. Mr J. S. Howard is the Surgeon Superintendent.

The *Kenilworth*, 537 tons, was taking in cargo for this colony, and as large quantities were ready, she is reported to sail certainly the last week in March.

The *Lord Raglan*, convict ship, was expected to leave early in March. Dr Bowers is the Navy Surgeon in charge.

Deputy Commissary General Williams, was in London waiting orders to embark for this colony.

We are glad to find that prices of our staple articles of product are improving an advance of 1½ per lb , was expected at the February Wool Sales, and copper is quoted at £127.

We have again to regret the non-receipt of the Indian Mails, and owing to the great delay in the steamer's arrival,

This is a good example of the news that circulated in the newspapers, this piece being from April 1858. What interested readers was prices of raw materials, comings and goings and India. The arrival of every ship is noted in the papers. The arrival of Emma Eugenia that ignited such fierce controversy is ringed.

philanthropy. They knew Ireland and understood the plight of Irish Catholics, both at home in Ireland and in Western Australia and actively helped them. They related to these people.

This active philanthropy can be seen to have begun with the arrival twelve years earlier, on 8th January 1846, of the barque *Elizabeth* which sailed into Fremantle carrying twenty seven 'Romanists'. The party included six 'Sisters of Mercy', nuns from Ireland. Rev. Dr. Brady had said earlier to his small Catholic flock that he would arrange for them to come but to the majority of the population their arrival was unexpected and unwelcome. Their mission was to serve the isolated Catholic flock. The Sisters, in particular, were active and outspoken in a manner considered unseemly for ladies. Of course, this was before the arrival of hundreds of Irish girls and convicts. This "inundation of Jesuits" was abused in the street and feared as a danger to children who might be seduced by their alien doctrine. Looking back on this time, the sisters recalled the deep resentment to their work but they said that they didn't go there to convert the influential but to care for the poor who were mainly, in their own words, "*the bog-Irish and black savages*". Thomas and Eliza became among the Sisters' greatest friends and benefactors. They understood their mission as, of course, they had been brought up among the bog Irish themselves.

The term 'bog Irish' may be considered offensive today and was probably meant to be offensive then. It crops up frequently in contemporary reports and even the Sisters used it, seemingly throwing it back in their detractors' faces.

The 1848 Western Australia census which showed the population to be 4,622 also asked people's religion and 337 people claimed to be Catholics. Nearly all the 337 were Irish and poor but the Sisters of Mercy were used to helping and comforting people such as these at home in Ireland. Later, the Sisters said they could name the number of influential Catholics on the fingers of one hand, and actually named the five. Two of the five were couples so their list was, in fact, seven individuals. The first on their list was, ironically, the man sent out from Britain to be Colonial Secretary of Western Australia, Richard Madden. He was not only Catholic, but Irish too. He reported back that,

> On my arrival in the Swan River Settlement I found Dr. Brady contending single handed against the entire local government, every member of which, with two exceptions, was bitterly opposed to Catholicity.

Also listed were Charlotte and Patrick Marmion who owned The Emerald Isle Hotel in Fremantle and who put the Sisters up for their first few days. Also in the five was Captain John Scully, formerly of the 80th Foot Regiment, who had whaling interests, was a farmer and magistrate in the Toodyay district and Bernard Smith who was a government Staff Clerk and much later a member of Perth City Council. In the middle of their list were Thomas and Eliza Little who were described as the founders of Dardanup. This is one of the very few surviving references to name Eliza and it is significant that she and Thomas are jointly named as founders of Dardanup. Eliza Little and Charlotte Marmion were the only two wives whose names were joined with their husbands as influential. The Sisters were not allowed to socialise with those outside their community for fear of being tainted by the ways of the world. Pastoral visits were to carry out their mission of mercy and not to make friends. Despite this, the sisters' surviving correspondence names six "true friends"; the Smiths, Marmions and Littles.

Eliza's help with the Sisters of Mercy was well publicised and she appeared to have had no fear of anti-Catholic repercussions. In 1847 and 1848 it was published in the Perth Gazette that she had donated £5 to their cause, a substantial amount. Twice in 1851 the Sisters ran a raffle for items that had been donated to them; a musical box, a rosewood workbox and a suite of Maltese filigree silver ornaments. Mrs Little was one of the ladies in different parts of the Colony from whom tickets could be bought. One of these advertisements is shown overleaf.

By the early 1850s there were Catholic churches in three main centres of population; Perth, Fremantle and Albany. At the end of 1852 Thomas and Eliza gave 50 acres of land at Dardanup for the building of a church, monastery and school. It would be the first Catholic church out in a rural area and may have been part of a long term plan of Thomas to create a Catholic enclave in that area, a safe haven. The foundation stone was laid by Bishop Salvado in March 1854, surrounded by about thirty parishioners who had travelled to mark the event. Cannon Martelli, an assistant priest who gave a sermon sums up the location and spirit of the occasion.

"It was in the midst of the woods, under the canopy of heaven that the ceremony was accomplished, not with pomp, but with great spiritual joy."

Despite the donation of £25 by the Bishop, the laying of the foundation stone and some preliminary work, progress came to a halt due to lack of funds and it was about this time that Thomas donated 100,000 bricks and 50 bushels of calcimine, the equivalent of cement, so the building could commence.

RAFFLE
This advertisement explains the causes dear to the hearts of the Sisters of Mercy and Eliza Little.
Mrs Charles Clifton was the former Maria Glynn

164

The church's first priest arrived in January 1856 and he put together a new committee to raise money to finish the work. By loaning £20 Thomas led the small group of donors who saved the day by raising £65 to finish the job. This was to be paid back as soon as the church could afford it over three years. Work then progressed and the Church of the Immaculate Conception was opened in October 1857. It was small, only 44' x 18' (13.5m x 5.5m). All this went on right in the middle of the staged construction of Dardanup Park and even Rev. Wollaston, in his diary, admitted that the Littles had made a *"sacrificial donation"*. Thomas' donation of bricks, which were being hand made for Dardanup Park, may have been a reason why the house was not completed until 1858. But the Littles continued to support the Catholic Church and the Sisters in building their own small convent in Perth and several schools around the Colony.

The first three priests lived at Dardanup Park with the Littles. The second priest, Fr. Garrido, was an inspirational man of missionary zeal whose reputation as a legendary adventurer preceded him. He had just returned from a 1000 mile (1600km) tour, on horseback, as far as the lead mines at Geraldine, far to the north-west. He was determined to take God's presence to the people and this he continued to do in his new parish. He was never idle. He oversaw the completion of the church but even before this he held Mass every Sunday. He set up a choir. During every week he visited his people no matter the distance, weather, terrain or rivers to cross. He and his horse would just appear out of the bush at the most remote stations, to say Mass, conduct baptisms, even marriages. Fr. Garrido was inspirational and Thomas believed he laid the foundations of the church as firmly as that first stone, laid four years earlier. Thomas' letter to Fr. Garrido on his departure tells us as much about Thomas Little as it does about Fr. Garrido. By his own hand Thomas demonstrates that he was an educated and erudite man.

Dardanup. 12th July 1858

Dear Father Garrido

It has pleased Almighty God that your ministry to the little flock at this place should cease from this day; such at least is the will of the Bishop and I trust we shall ever consider our Bishop's will as the will of God in all things pertaining to the government of the church – and therefore to it we bow.

For the good you have done to the honour of God and of His little flock, I regret I cannot offer you a more substantial testimony than a few fitting words, but I know you seek not any such testimony and you look for reward of your works only where you have so often and so well taught us to look for ours, in Heaven. There then I pray that your reward, dear father, may be great indeed, and I am sure that in this fervent prayer I am joined by every member of my household and every member of your bereaved flock. And that our Merciful God may guide you in safety to whatever part of the world you may now be destined for, is the further prayer of

Your affectionate friend in Jesus Christ

Thomas Little

P.S. I take the liberty to enclose you a copy of a letter I wrote to Dr. Serra yesterday and which you are welcome to use as you like. TL

Because of the delay in building the church with its school, the first school opened in the Littles' own house. Its teacher was John Clancy, a 'Ticket of Leave Man'. He was a convict who was given parole because of his good behaviour. Tickets came with restrictions such as the man having to be in employment and being prohibited from leaving the area. He had to carry his Ticket at all times. Despite being desperate for manual labourers, some people refused to employ ex-convicts and with good reason, as they saw it. In 1854 there were 243 Ticket of Leave men in the Bunbury area and over half of them (128) were re-convicted in that year and sent back to the convict depot. Reconvictions included misdemeanours such as incompetence, unreliability, insolence and drunkenness. But here was John Clancy, a Ticket Man, employed by Thomas Little in a responsible position as a teacher. By his name, Clancy would seem to have been Irish and, no doubt, a Catholic too. Between 1863 and 1869 Thomas employed seven Ticket Men and William employed four. Many men were sentenced to deportation for what would now be considered trivial crimes and the Littles gave them a second chance. Unfortunately, Thomas' trust appears to have been misplaced in this case and Clancy was reconvicted for inappropriate behaviour with a young girl in his charge.

This takes us to the other strand of the Littles' generosity; helping the Irish poor. In broad terms Thomas gave many an Irish immigrant family 100 acres. This was not a pure gift. Some say it was based on an improving lease whereby the tenant had to erect a house, clear the land and erect fencing. It seems that, perhaps, half their crop had to be paid to the Littles in lieu of rent. But it is also said that the Littles supported newcomers financially during their early years of hard work and no income. Whatever the detail, these were very lucky families.

Domestic Sayings and Doings.

We have been much gratified during the past week, to witness so lively a response to a late call upon the sympathies of this community, in aid of a recently widowed lady, on whose part we beg to tender her heartfelt thanks to those charitable persons who have so generously contributed to relieve her necessity. We are requested to convey her deep sense of gratitude for so much disinterested kindness, coming, as it does, from perfect strangers, few of whom knew more than the name of her late husband, affording convincing proof that the true object of charity has only to present itself, to be at once appreciated and adopted by this small but benevolent community.

We hear it is the intention of Government to allow brandy to be taken out of the bonded stores under certain restrictions, free of duty, for the purpose of assisting the manufacture of wine. The present vintage is expected to be a bad one, and this will be a considerable boon. Those only however, can be benefitted, who are large vine growers, as the indulgence will be only extended to those parties who possess two acres of vineyard.

The *William Pope*, returned from Albany and the southern ports on Monday last. After making a trip to the northward, this vessel will also be also laid on for the diggings.

A number of Irish emigrants, who came out last year to Mr Little's of Australind, are about proceeding to the gold country in the *Louisa*, and we hear that other laboring men are also intending to leave the Leschenault. The *Evergreen* takes nineteen passengers.

Some specimens of quartz, thought to contain a large portion of gold, were brought in from the Canning, in the early part of the week. They have been submitted to examination but not been found to realise the expectations of those who found them, although offering indications of the precious metal. Our fellow-townsman, Mr Abcott, has exhibited a specimen of Melbourne gold, containing rather more than eleven sovereigns, brought in the *Louisa*, by Captain Douglass.

DOMESTIC SAYINGS AND DOINGS
The Perth Gazette of 12th March 1852 gives examples of what interested the local folk.
Helping a widow
The poor wine crop
Making a fortune from gold.
But the item of most interest is the reference, near the bottom, to Irish emigrants who came to Thomas Little's land. Is this evidence of his direct help?

How many received this enormous benefit is not known nor how they got themselves to Western Australia. He may have encouraged them to come by contacts in Britain or through the church but there is little evidence of this. The news report on the previous page could be taken to infer that men travelled from Ireland directly to the Littles' estate but it is not evidence that Thomas sought them. One of them is known to have been a porter in London, doing heavy, poorly paid work, which would not have allowed the man to save to pay for his passage. It is known that landlords in Ireland sometimes paid the fare to get rid of surplus tenants, but not usually to Australia which was an expensive journey. It raises the question of why Eliza's brother, Patrick Lally, didn't come. He was in London at this time, they were in touch and surely his sister would have welcomed him.

One of the Irish families the Littles helped was James Maguire and his wife Elizabeth Carberry. James was from Limerick but Elizabeth was from Galway and she had come to Western Australia on the *Palestine*, arriving in Fremantle on 28th April 1853 after five months at sea. She was one of 32 orphan girls from Mountbellew workhouse, 23 miles north of Loughrea. You can picture the conversation Elizabeth and Thomas and Eliza had when she first arrived at Dardanup. They had a lot in common but she had left Galway nearly thirty years after Thomas and Eliza had last seen their homeland. She would have told them of the Great Famine and all the other changes that had occurred since then. Thomas would have taken a particular interest in getting them settled in and shared their optimism that, after Ireland, anything had to be better. The Maguires did well as only three years later James Maguire appears as one of the major contributors to the building of the church.

It is interesting to look at Thomas and Eliza's home, Dardanup Park, at this time, say during the summer of 1857/8, just after the building of the church close-by had finished. Thomas and Eliza lived there with Thomas Jr. and William who were both still unmarried. The final phase of house building was continuing so it was a building site with brick-makers, sawyers and builders, perhaps many living round about during the construction. A good number of these are bound to have been Irish Catholics. Farm workers were tending the crops and vines. Eliza had her servants who needed to help with the cooking for so many visitors. And was she responsible for cooking for many of the workers too? The resident visitor was Fr. Garrido, when he was not on his travels. In the cottage at the back was John Clancy, the school teacher, but at least the school had by now moved to a building with the new church so local children were not coming and going. Were the Chinese labourers sleeping in the cellars at this time? If so, they would have gathered outside in any spare time they had. Then animals; there would have been horses for personal and work use, probably dogs and the inevitable chickens running around. There would have been constant comings and goings of builders' supplies, and other deliveries and social calls from neighbours. This image takes us back to the 1821 census in Carraroe, and the Little's family home in Ireland. It shows the Littles with several visitors – an open house, open to all, and cheek by jowl with the property next door, owned by the man who may have been the employer of some of the Little sons. So it was here in Dardanup, in sharp contrast to our fenced-in and isolated modern families. But all this hubbub and goings on was home to the Littles; it was the only sort of life they'd ever known.

In the six years from 1848 to 1854 the number of Catholics in the surrounding district grew from 31 to 249, many of whom must have been beneficiaries of the Littles. Today, all these years later, the area round Dardanup has one of the highest concentrations of Catholics in Western Australia.

Religious differences had not stopped Rev. Wollaston selling his Dardanup land to the Littles when he moved to Albany and eight years later, in 1856, he recorded a visit back to his old home and the Littles' partly built new house. This was just as the Littles were making their second large donation towards the building of the new Catholic Church. Despite his active anti-Catholicism, often expressed robustly in his diary, Wollaston still respected the Littles and one can read in this entry an admiration for what they had achieved and at what cost.

> *"Tuesday 11th March 1856. To Dardanup – to dinner. I had seen Little and promised to take him in on my way.*
>
> *Little has a capital brick house of two storeys and if his plan could be carried out it would be by far the best in the district. The whole neighbourhood is now under cultivation to a great extent and many small homesteads are now occupied, I believe, entirely by Roman Catholics whom Little has gathered around him and for whom he has built a handsome chapel, but he complained he had no money to go on with it. I suspect the*

truth is that his Bishop has screwed out of him all he can and that the poor man is in much straitened circumstances. I could see many indications of this. The wheat has not been above an average this year. Fires most extensive had destroyed great quantities of fencing."

Wednesday 12th March. Took cordial leave of the Littles.

Wollaston rode on to the Cliftons at Australind. His diary entry is an interesting contrast to the straitened circumstances but optimism he reported at the Littles' new house.

"Difficulties thicken on the old man (Waller Clifton). He is eaten up by hangers-on . . Rosamel mortgaged and he wants to wheedle something out of the new Governor that he may go and live at Perth but it would only involve him in greater difficulties. Australind, sandy, dull and wretched. Company's buildings on the hill burnt to ashes and those below in ruins."

The time after their new house was completed, in 1858, must have been the best of times for the Littles but it was to be short lived. They borrowed to build their dream home and farming estate and they gave a great deal to their charitable causes and it is unlikely that they ever gained the financial security they planned. But the Littles didn't judge life's successes in purely financial terms. As they entered their 60s and perhaps thought life would get easier they suffered a series of heavy blows; financial and personal.

WESTERN AUSTRALIA

CHAPTER 12

FALL

The financial blows saw the collapse of Thomas' income and loss of his property. The personal blows were the deaths of Eliza and their son, William. In fact the timing of their acute financial problems is such that worry about this may have been a factor in Eliza's death.

Firstly, the wine harvests of 1862, the year of his great success in London, and 1863 were lost, almost completely, and Thomas' vines destroyed. This was probably due to drought, or perhaps blight. He would have had his earlier vintages to sell but by 1866 he had nothing and his creditors wanted £2500 – an enormous sum. It is most likely that he was forced to let Dardanup Park go to his creditors. Can you imagine the scene as he, perhaps with Eliza looking over his shoulder, signed that document that ended their dreams? Somehow he got through this and kept the right to continue to live in Dardanup Park.

The greatest blow to Thomas must have been his loss of Eliza in the same year. She died on 24th November 1866 at their home at Dardanup Park, at the age of 69 years and 6 months, to be precise. She died of a heart attack so probably with little warning. Could the stress of their financial problems have been a factor in her death? The team of the entrepreneurial Thomas and his lively, sociable, supportive and hard working Eliza was shattered. Shock caused by the suddenness of her demise may have been the reason why the notice of her death did not appear in the newspapers for nearly two months. The announcement of her death also tells of the death Francis Clifton, the son of Maria Glynn, a month after Eliza's death. It is unlikely that, at the time, Thomas noticed that he had been 'promoted' to Esq, an honour long overdue considering his public works, philanthropy and land-holdings.

Births, Marriages, and Deaths.

BIRTHS.

JAMES—At Perth, on the 10th inst., the wife of Mr. E. S. JAMES, of a daughter.

GULL.—At Guildford, on the morning of the New Year, Mrs. GULL, of a son.

MARRIAGES.

MITCHELL—CHURCHYARD.—At St. Matthew's Church, Guildford, by the Rev. H. B. Grimaldi, on the 10th January instant—JOSEPH MITCHELL, of Guildford, to HARRIET ELIZA CHURCHYARD, of Perth.

LEEDER—MORRELL.—At St. James' Church, Northam, on Thursday, Nov. 22, by the Rev. C. Clay, WILLIAM GEORGE, eldest son of the late WILLIAM HENRY LEEDER, ESQ., to HANNAH EMILY, eldest daughter of FRED. MORRELL, ESQ.

DEATHS.

LITTLE.—At Dardanup, on the 24th November, 1866, aged 69 years and 6 months, ELIZA, the beloved wife of THOMAS LITTLE, ESQ., J.P. R.I.P.

CLIFTON.—At Guildford, on the 30th December, FRANCIS DUDLEY G., infant son of CHARLES H. CLIFTON, Esq.; aged 6 months and a few days.

MEARES.—At York, on the 17th inst., RICHARD GAMBLE BOYCE MEARES, second son of the late R. G. MEARES, Esq., formerly Captain in the 2nd Life Guards; aged 47 years.

Near the bottom of this column in the "Perth Enquirer and Commercial News" is the notice of the death of Eliza Little, two months after the event.

The official State death record names her as Eliza Little (née Lally).

In the same notice is the death of the son of Maria Glynn and Charles Clifton.

Two and a half years later Thomas suffered a second tragedy with the loss of his younger son, William, who died on 17th June 1869 at only 36 years of age and leaving his wife, Helena, and three small children under the age of six. He died of cancer which explains the death notice saying not only that he died prematurely but after a protracted and painful illness. William seems to have been, perhaps less of an extrovert, the quieter of Thomas and Eliza's two sons, the family man, probably just getting on with his life. He seems to have farmed his own land, had his horses and played cricket. But still a hundred mourners were at his funeral so he had made an impact. The obituary appeared in the news columns of the *Perth Enquirer and Commercial News* so was not written by the family. Only his father and brother are mentioned in the obituary so was there no thought for his grieving wife? At the time of his death, William and his family were living with his father at Dardanup Park, perhaps because in his final days he was unable to support them and could be better cared for there.

Mr. William Little of Dardanup, died prematurely last week, after a protracted and painful illness. The funeral of the deceased gentleman took place at Dardanup on Thursday, 10th inst., and was attended by about one hundred people, amongst whom were most of our principal inhabitants, who, accompanying the corpse of the departed to its last earthly dwelling, thus testified their esteem for his memory, and their sympathy with his bereaved father and brother. His good works follow him : may he rest in peace.
17th June.

The notice of death of William Little in the "Perth Enquirer and Commercial News".

Today, deaths can be delayed. In an emergency an ambulance can be called with paramedics with the means of bringing even people with heart attacks back to normal life. It is to be hoped that Thomas was at home when Eliza died but he must have been desperate, maybe alone, as he could do nothing to save her. What does one do in such circumstances? He could have called nearby workers or leave her alone and run to neighbours. But all this would have been in the knowledge that his life had changed for ever and his soulmate since childhood was gone. Was it after this that William and his family moved to Dardanup Park? William's was a slower, more painful and expected death but no less sad for that. There were no effective painkillers, just loving care.

With Thomas now on his own, 1868 saw the start of a worldwide economic depression, affecting Britain and India on which Western Australia was so dependant for trade and income. The market for horses and railway sleepers collapsed. Matters were made worse for Western Australia by the cessation of the arrival of convict labour and, as a consequence, loss of funds from Britain. Convicts had been received into Western Australia from 1850 to overcome the shortage of labour. They had built the road south from Perth, for example, and it was hoped that this would open up the area for greater trade. It would make it easier to get goods to Perth, rather than by sea. In 1867 a horse mail service had opened along this road. But none of this helped and in future the labour for such projects would have to be paid for through taxation. This was a worldwide depression but higher taxation and higher labour costs in a marginal economy such as Western Australia could only make matters worse.

Thomas was still a JP (Justice of the Peace) and no doubt his reputation and his dignity helped him to keep above the worst of this, perhaps just surviving on rent from his tenants. One of Thomas' last formal events at Dardanup Park took place in February 1870 when the recently appointed Governor of Western Australia had been on a lengthy tour of the colony, calling on the major houses and industries. Nearly twenty years after a previous Governor had dined with Thomas and Eliza at Belvidere this Governor had lunch at Dardanup Park, demonstrating that Thomas had remained an important local figure. When the tour culminated with a banquet for sixty eminent persons Thomas Little was honoured with a place at the top table.

But there followed several years of devastating drought and in 1871 dust storms devastated crops, leaving many people without food or seed for next year. In July 1872 a group of Dardanup residents, 28 in all, put a bulk petition to the Colonial Secretary for aid after Red Rust blight had completely destroyed the wheat crop. Thomas was among the petitioners. Only two cases, of the 28, were successful. One was transferred to Perth Poor House and the other was offered a bag of flour a month because he had twelve children to support. A report by an aide to the Colonial Secretary sums up the battle everybody had been fighting since the beginning of the Settlement.

> "If Government was to subsidise and support every and any of the colonists (not an agriculturalist) who had failed at his business, to a certain extent speculative, how would the revenue stand? Agriculture, except as an industry outside more important ones, is, in this Colony, a mistake and, in the hands of the sort of farmers we have here, a delusion. It may seem hard, but I cannot rid myself of such an opinion."

Instead of aid, some settlers were told to take out loans on their land but Thomas' land was already mortgaged. Some were told to take jobs as labourers until things improved but Thomas was 72 years old. The Colonial Secretary saw this as an opportunity to rationalise agriculture by eliminating small subsistence farmers, rather than

Thomas Little

A photograph of Thomas Little taken in his later years. There is no photograph of Eliza, perhaps because photography had not developed and was not readily available before her death in 1866.

"wasting money subsidising small farms on charity". The list of petitioners had a hand written note against some names and against Thomas Little was written, *"not a case for public relief"*. It must have been an incredibly sad time for Thomas as he and so many of his tenants and the people he had helped had their hopes dashed.

One of the petitioners was James Maguire. When aid was first being given, he was doing well enough to be refused it because he had money owing to him. Now it was unlikely that his debtors could pay him but he was still denied relief despite this.

Oh dear, rationalisation of small farm plots and loss of homes and livelihoods; echoes of Ireland must have been ringing in their ears. But these weren't the 6 acre plots of Ireland. A hundred acres was considered small in Australia. The argument for rationalisation of small farms was illogical when confronted with the fact that many large farming estates were failing too. Not only did Thomas' venture collapse but it was in 1874 that Prinsep's business, which Thomas had started nearly 40 years previously, failed. It was being run by Henry Prinsep, one of Charles Prinsep's sons, and not even he could make a go of it. He was exporting timber and continuing the breeding of horses for India but horses, which up until 1870 had been selling for £30, were, in 1871, selling for £17. In 1872 a horse might only fetch £5.

In 1875 the grand plan of Australind was finally and officially abandoned, having been falling apart for years. Australind's demise was even commented on by Rev. Wollaston as far back as 1856, as we have seen, but it also typified many of the colony's problems. So often the soil quality was poor and occasionally the weather turned against farms of all sizes with floods, drought, sandstorms and bush fires which destroyed all that had been built up. If the whaling industry had failed, the timber industry had failed and agriculture was a mistake (as suggested in the report to the Colonial Secretary), what was the economy to be built on? Despite its vast areas of land, Western Australia was dependent on flour imports throughout the Victorian era. Some historians have criticised Thomas and Eliza for the failure of their enterprise but in the light of events outside their control, and their generosity, this criticism is hardly fair. Success in life cannot only be measured in financial terms and they had made many choices that demonstrated that financial wealth was not where their priorities lay.

By 1874, Thomas' only surviving son had left, and who could blame him. It must have then been a particular sadness for Thomas when Thomas Jr. left to establish and manage the vast and remote Meka Station, 370 miles north of Perth where he became managing partner with two men from Fremantle. Meka Station covered 904,000 acres, 1,400 square miles, 3650 sq Km. Thomas Jr. set about installing hundreds of miles of fencing and introducing tens of thousands of sheep, cattle and some horses. His partners remained in Fremantle so Thomas Jr. was up there alone with his station hands. This might appear a strange and lonely existence but he was involved in many activities in the region, particularly in his role as JP. He had seen the struggle to make a success of the area around the old Swan River Settlement, over many years, and now saw the large holdings and grand families failing so must have thought he had a better chance elsewhere.

So Thomas was left alone. Where was the rest of his family? If he'd had a dream that his family would take over where he left off and inherit the family home and business it was now dashed.

Thomas Jr. was nearly 500 miles away. Maria, who had fallen out with her foster parents 25 years previously, was now on better terms but that didn't extend to visiting. She had lived locally for only four years but then moved, eventually settling in Perth where her husband became Superintendent of Perth jail. Helena, William's widow and Thomas' daughter in law, had probably moved to Perth and although she still had her husband's land at Dardanup it was held as security for a debt and of very little value to her. She had Thomas' three grandchildren, Elizabeth Mary who was 11 at this time, Annie, 8 years old and William John who was 6.

Thomas died on 5th November 1877, at the age of 77. He got a very complimentary, if brief, report in the local papers, rather than the usual paid-for classified announcement. It was the biggest funeral Bunbury had ever seen and important people of all classes and denominations travelled from far and wide to pay their respects to a pioneer colonist and highly respected resident. There are no surviving graves for Thomas, or Eliza or William, all of whom one would expect to have been buried in Dardanup cemetery. But Thomas' funeral parade was in Bunbury so perhaps he was buried there. The Catholic cemetery in Bunbury was swallowed up in a dune blowout and his mortal remains are most likely deep down in their adopted country.

Thomas and Eliza's fortune had come and gone. It was probably only ever illusory as even the building of their magnificent house was based on hope for the future. They left no substantial sum to their heirs. And what of those heirs in later years?

Thomas Jr. had his flocks decimated by the drought of 1891 but built them up again until illness forced him to move to Perth for treatment. He lived with Helena, his sister-in-law, who nursed him through his final days, as she had done for William. When his end came in April 1900 his funeral was a Solemn Requiem Mass in the Catholic Cathedral in Perth and, as at his father's passing, it was attended by many people from all walks of life, including Henry Prinsep from the early days. There were several representatives of the Little and Clifton families at his funeral, showing that the various branches of Thomas and Eliza's family stayed in touch, including the family that Maria Glynn had married in to. Thomas Jr. was greatly respected and left a reputation similar to that of his father, for kindness and generosity to bushmen and aborigines.

Helena died in 1916 in Kalgoorlie, a remote gold mining town, 450 miles to the east of Dardanup, on the edge of the desert where she had gone to be with her son in law who was working on the building of the Trans-Australian railway. And what of William and Helena's children, Thomas and Eliza's grandchildren? Elizabeth (Bessie Grundy) was a Sub Post Mistress in Perth and died in 1911. Annie, was to become a Catholic nun in 1888, known as Sister Mary Augustine, Mistress of Novices in Fremantle and a music teacher at St Joseph's Convent, Northam. That would have pleased Thomas and Eliza. Their only grandson, William, was to die of thirst in 1892 after getting lost on an expedition in the outback with friends.

Thomas had time to look back on his life. He lived to a good age and his final illness lasted several weeks so he knew, or hoped, he was on his way to a better place. If he was not too hard on himself, he must have looked back with satisfaction on the risks he had taken in leaving Ireland, on achieving success, despite the odds, in India and then leaving that for the new venture in Western Australia. He would have looked back on the many happy times spent with family and friends and the very sad times, especially the loss of his beloved Eliza and several children. There is plenty of evidence that he and Eliza shared their success by helping others in Australia and, as that was their character, in India too. Adopting Maria, their friends' daughter, was an act of love typical of them both. The wealth and contentment they received from their strivings was simply a roof over their head, a meal on the table and helping others. *"Riches they heed not, nor man's empty praise. God was their inheritance, now and always",* to paraphrase an old Irish melody.

Thomas and Eliza Little brought nothing into this world and had nothing to take with them when they left it. In a tough, pioneer community they were widely known and respected for their generosity, philanthropy, hospitality and fair dealing. They are still remembered by the descendants of the Irish Catholic immigrants who they supported. So often history remembers royalty and officials. It is Governor Generals, the first Postmaster, the High Court Judge who are the sort of people who have statues and appear on bank notes. But just as important are Thomas and Eliza Little who never held high office but are remembered for establishing their part of the Colony and giving it a character that still remains today.

Thomas' signature is taken from the frontispiece of his gardening book, shown on page 140. The obituary says he suffered for several weeks. He gave this book to his friend during this time, perhaps indicating that he knew his time on this earth was short and was handing on some treasured possessions to friends.

Obituary

It is with unfeigned regret that we record this month the demise of THOMAS LITTLE ESQ. JP. of Dardanup. After a lingering illness of several weeks duration, during which he bore with Christian patience the suffering incidental to his complaint, he, yesterday morning at half past nine, breathed his last.

In Mr LITTLE'S death, the Catholic Church in Western Australia has lost one of her most faithful members. Ardently attached to the faith in which he believed, his relations with his church were those of affection and filial obedience. His conduct evinced an unwavering esteem for her authority and unfailing reverence for her laws. Constant in the discharge of all those obligations which her laws impose, and exact in the fulfilment of his religious duties, his example was a reproach to the careless and an encouragement of the good amongst whom his lot was cast.

Arriving in this colony at a time when the very name of Catholic was almost unknown, when not even a site had been marked for a Catholic Church and no priest had yet set foot on Western Australian soil; Mr LITTLE lived to see the Catholic faith attain that degree of strength, extent and influence it now enjoys. The contrast of what had been and what was, was a familiar thought with him in his declining years. The success of the Church was greater than he had ever hoped to see, and it was a solace to him to speak and a pleasure to think, of the subject so near to his heart. Could services rendered give any one a right to rejoice in the prosperity of the Church, as in that of something personal to himself, Mr LITTLE might well claim the privilege. Catholicity in the Southern Districts owes, we are almost tempted to say, under God, the present position of Mr LITTLE'S efforts more than to ought else.

The short notice we have received before going to press, forbids us to write much that we would like to pen. We now only repeat the Church's prayer for the departed – Requiscat in pace – an act of charity in which we ask our Catholic readers to join

These are two of the obituaries of Thomas Little.
The smaller one was in The "Perth Enquirer and Commercial News" of 14th November 1877 and in other newspapers.
The main one appeared in the Catholic Record of November 1877.

180

Thomas' church, previously the Church of the Immaculate Conception, was renamed the Thomas Little Memorial Hall in 1979. This photo shows it after its restoration in 2019.

ACKNOWLEDGEMENTS

AND

BIBLIOGRAPHY

I have written about Thomas and Eliza in narrative form as a story for my grandchildren. Its aim is to paint a picture of what life was like for their ancestors and how it varied from their lives today. This is why it brings in situations from other lives, if they help to paint that picture. It is meant to be an easy and enjoyable read, rather than a strict timetable of dates and events. Most of the information the story contains comes from secondary sources which are sometimes conflicting.

My first thanks must go to Linda Sue Strand (née Little) who started this whole project. She read *The Leaving of Loughrea* and saw common threads with her family; Loughrea, Lally, Brett and Swan River. She emailed to ask if this was just a coincidence or of interest. It was certainly of interest.

ILLUSTRATIONS

Most illustrations are readily available on the internet and most are more than 150 years old. Where possible I have stated their provenance and credited the artists. I have not always been successful in finding the creators of more modern works and I should be pleased to hear from anybody who claims rights to these illustrations.

IRELAND

I am indebted to Kieran Jordan for an enormous amount of help in providing core information on the Littles. He is an expert on Irish history and on the east Galway area and has investigated sources I would never have found and helped greatly with impressions of local life at this time.

The Leaving of Loughrea – An Irish Family in the Great Famine, by Stephen Lally. Brief descriptions of life in Ireland are taken from the more detailed research carried out for this book.

The British Library in London holds the original detailed records of all East India Company personnel.

> 'Depot Registers' of the East India Company Army. These provide personal and physical details, occupation, residence, of every recruit, at the time of recruitment.
>
> Artillery, January 1820 – December 1830: IOR: L/MIL/9/30
>
> Infantry, January 1816 – December 1826: IOR: L/MIL/9/41

The Journals of the Irish Family History Society have several articles, between 1995 and 2001, on Irishmen who joined the East India Company Army.

INDIA

Thanks to Linda Sue Strand who had already done some online family history research in British India and set down the markers that I could follow in greater depth.

FIBIS – The Families in British India Society which has a comprehensive database and fibiwiki. Particularly helpful is their publication *Researching Ancestors in the East India Company Armies* by Peter A Bailey.

The British Library which has an incredible library of original East India Company records from the earliest times, in which every man is recorded year by year, along with enlistment and embarkation records, etc. It also has a large collection of contemporary newspapers.

Embarkation Lists give details of when and how soldiers sailed and whether wives were with them.
Mar 1816 – Jun 1824: IOR: L/MIL/9/99

Muster Rolls & Casualty Returns. Annual returns on each soldier; rank, battalion and company, casualties, etc., 1824 – 1837. IOR: L/MIL/10/145 – 158

Register of EIC European Soldiers in Bengal. Personal details incl. place of origin in roughly alphabetical order by year of arrival, 1793 – 1839. IOR: L/MIL/10/122

The ship's log of Macqueen. IOR/L/MAR/B/11B

Bengal Past and Present – the Journal of The Calcutta Historical Society, 1907 – 2007. Vol.108, 1989, an article on The Prinsep Family by A C Staples of MI Teachers College, Western Australia

On the Population and Mortality of Calcutta by Lt Col. W H Sykes F R S Published in The Journal of The Statistical Society of London, March 1845, Vol. 8, No.1. Available at jstor.org

WESTERN AUSTRALIA

I received great help from a number of people in Western Australia who have kindly provided an enormous and invaluable list of references to the Littles that I could not have found myself.

The following sources have been used to create this story.

Trove is the Australian National Library's website and portal to all historical newspapers and content in libraries, museums and cultural institutions. Its newspaper archive has been the backbone of dates and events in my story and some of the illustrations are from Trove. Nearly everything I have searched on Trove is available and downloadable. It's easy to use. It has proved vital. Nearly all stories were covered by all the early Western Australia newspapers.

The Leschenault Peninsula by Irma Walter. Published by Harvey History Online, 2017. History of the strip of land covering Thomas Little's purchase of it and their life at Belvidere.

Women out of Their Sphere by Anne McLay, 1992. The History of the Sisters of Mercy in Western Australia. The Littles are covered on pages 37, 45-6, 56-62, 77, 182.

A Friend Indeed by George Russo, 1995. Biography of Louisa Clifton of Australind, Western Australia, 1814 – 1880. This is based on the diaries of Louisa Clifton. The Littles are covered on pages10, 150 – 167, 185, 280 -281.

Thomas Little at Dardanup. A university thesis by Ruth McGrath, School of Social History, November 1986. 17 typed pages. An excellent background to the Littles with useful bibliography.

The Australind Journals of Marshall Waller Clifton 1840 – 1861 by P Barnes, J M Cameron & H A Willis.

The Wollaston Journals, edited by Helen Walker Mann, 2006. These diaries of Rev. John Wollaston are quoted in several other sources but some quotes come direct from this edition.

Mary Amelia Wollaston: A Life of Amusing Contrasts by Helen Wallace. Taken from Amelia Wollaston's diaries and gives a good idea of tribulations of early settlers on arrival. Pages 510 – 522

Excellent Connections, A History of Bunbury, Western Australia, 1836 - 1990 by Anthony J Barker and Maxine Laurie, 1991. The Littles are covered on pages 7, 12, 29 – 31, 57, 65, 75-6, 84, 87.

Flynn of the Ferguson, A Documented Family History of Henry Stanes Flynn by Norm Flynn, 1903. Published by Australind Family History Society. Flynn was a recipient of land from Thomas Little. Much information on the Littles but also on Australind and the rift between Littles and Cliftons.

Reminiscences of Fifty Years Residence in Western Australia by J T Reilly, 1903. Sections with personal memories of the Littles. Pages 4 – 5, 635 – 637.

Colonial Cousins - A Surprising History of Connections Between India and Australia by Joyce Westrip and Peggy Holroyde,. Interesting background to Prinsep and what drove his plans.

Early Days in Western Australia. The journal of the (Royal) Western Australian Historical Society which includes essays by various people of which the following refer to Thomas Little.

The Prinsep Estate in Western Australia by A C Staples MA. Vol.5 Pt.1

Birth of the Catholic Church in Dardanup by Dom William OSB. Vol.5 pt.6. 1960. Dom William quotes from original letters written by Thomas Little and "in his possession" but which perhaps were in the Catholic Archive at New Norcia.

Horse Racing in Western Australia by Mr S F Cusack Vol.2 pt.19 1936.

Local Heritage Survey description of Dardanup Park, 2016

Pioneer Aboriginal Mission: The Work of Wesleyan Missionary John Smithies in the Swan River Colony 1840-1855. McNair and Rumney.

Conflict and Commerce: American Whalers and the Western Australian Colonies 1826 – 1888. Paper by Martin Gibbs of the James Cook University. Published in 2000 in 'Great Circle' Vol 22, No. 2.

The Illustrated London News. Some interesting articles on the colony from an English perspective. The sketches of Perth, Fremantle, Culham and York and the India Mail are from here.

The Crystal Palace Foundation was a great help with information on the Industrial Exhibition of 1862. They guided me to the following two books:- *The World's Show* and *Recipients of Official Crystal Palace Medals* by Leslie Lewis Allen. Google Books has *The Official Catalogue of the International Exhibition 1862.*